SOPRINTENDENZA ARCHEOLO
PER L'ETRURIA MERIDIONA

# THE VILLA GIULIA
# NATIONAL ETRUSCAN MUSEUM

## SHORT GUIDE

*edited by*
Anna Maria Moretti Sgubini

«L'ERMA» di BRETSCHNEIDER      INGEGNERIA PER LA CULTURA

Soprintendenza Archeologica
per l'Etruria Meridionale
Museo Nazionale Etrusco di Villa Giulia

# The Villa Giulia National Etruscan Museum
## Short Guide

*Edited by*
Anna Maria Moretti Sgubini

*Texts*
Laura Ambrosini *[la]*
Maria Paola Baglione *[mpb]*
Maria Gilda Benedettini *[mgb]*
Irene Berlingò *[ib]*
Francesca Boitani *[fb]*
Tancredi Carunchio *[tc]*
Rita Cosentino *[rc]*
Filippo Delpino *[fd]*
Maria Anna De Lucia Brolli *[madlb]*
Anna Maria Moretti Sgubini *[amms]*
Maristella Pandolfini Angeletti *[mpa]*
Maria Antonietta Rizzo *[mar]*

*Editorial Office*
Maria Letizia Arancio

*Photographs*
Benito Fioravanti; archivio SAEM

*Graphics*
Leonardo Petolicchio, Alberto Villari

*Translation*
Graham Sells

ISBN 88-8265-012-X

An editorial achievment
«L'ERMA» di BRETSCHNEIDER, Rome
INGEGNERIA PER LA CULTURA, Rome

# Foreword

With the rich collections yielded by over a century's excavations and research carried out in the area of Southern Etruria, the Villa Giulia National Museum (*fig. 1*) offers an extensive and composite overview of Etruscan history and civilisation. The vast documentation providing a wealth of detail on the customs and habits, religion and ritual, fashions and tastes of a refined and cultivated society pieces together the vivid picture of a cosmopolitan people open to exchange and in direct contact with other Mediterranean peoples, but who succeeded in forging their own original culture. A good measure of the excellent quality achieved by the artists of Etruria is offered by a number of exquisite exhibits in the Museum including the *Caere* "Bride and bridegroom" Sarcophagus, the Veii Apollo, the Vulci Centaur, the *Pyrgi* high-relief and the Lo Scasato Apollo, to name but a few. Together with various other celebrated monuments, they provide exceptional evidence of Etruscan civilisation playing a leading role in the cultural scenario of Pre-Roman Italy.

The Museum is organised in various topographic sections dedicated to the most important centres of maritime Etruria. The cultural picture of these centres emerging here finds further illustration in the various local museums, while the historical background to the great Etruscan

Fig. 1. The Villa Giulia National Etruscan Museum.

sites is completed with the evidence of other Italic cultures flourishing in adjacent areas such as the Ager Faliscus and Ager Capenas, *Latium vetus* and Umbria, and with the material in various important repertories such as the Castellani and Barberini collections, deriving form 19th-century excavations in Etruria and made available to the Villa Giulia Museum in the period following on its foundation. In 1995-1996 a project was launched to reorganise the collections on a scientific basis and reopen extensive sections of the museum that had long been closed to the public. Thus 1997 saw the antiquities of *Pyrgi* displayed anew and innovatively, while June 1998 saw the reopening to the public of important evidence from the Faliscan and Capenas centres and 1999 completion of the museum arrangement with new display of antiquities from repertories such as the A. Castellani Collection, the various sets of exhibits from the Antiquarium together with material from the old Kircherian Museum fittingly exhibited and finally – the most recent acquisition – the Cima Pesciotti Collection. The arrangement of the Museum was also enhanced with the addition of three new sections

Fig. 2. Villa Giulia. The inner facade of the semicircular gallery after restoration.

dedicated, respectively, to Etruscan epigraphy, the history of the museum and Pope Julius' Villa and the changes it has gone through in the course of time. A fourth section is now planned, dedicated to Tarquinia – a centre hitherto unrepresented in the museum – which will be documented with one of the most celebrated examples of Etruscan painting, the tomb of the Funeral Couch. 1999 also saw completion of the delicate architectural restoration begun in 1998 in the 16th-century complex (*fig. 2*) where, as in the rest of the museum, work was also carried out to modernise the functional installations and safety systems. The Museum has now been made accessible to the disabled and equipped with various services for the public and a communications centre for didactic activities, and will soon be enjoying further extension to the neighbouring Villa Poniatowski (*fig. 3*). Thorough structural consolidation and architectural restoration is now being carried out on this latter villa, which will be housing the material from centres in *Latium vetus* and Umbria now displayed in rooms 32-35 in Villa Giulia, where in turn the antiquities from Veii will be exhibited in a more organic arrangement. Directly connected by a broad drive running below Villa Strohl-Fern, Villa Giulia and Villa Poniatowski will at last fulfil the long cherished ambition to create a great Etruscan museum complex for Rome.

ANNA MARIA MORETTI SGUBINI
Archaeological Superintendent
for Southern Etruria

Fig. 3. The crossroads between Via dell'Arco Oscuro (now Via di Villa Giulia) and the Via Flaminia in a print of 1757 (GIUSEPPE VASI, Pope Julius III's *Casino della Vigna*).

Plate I. Museum
services.

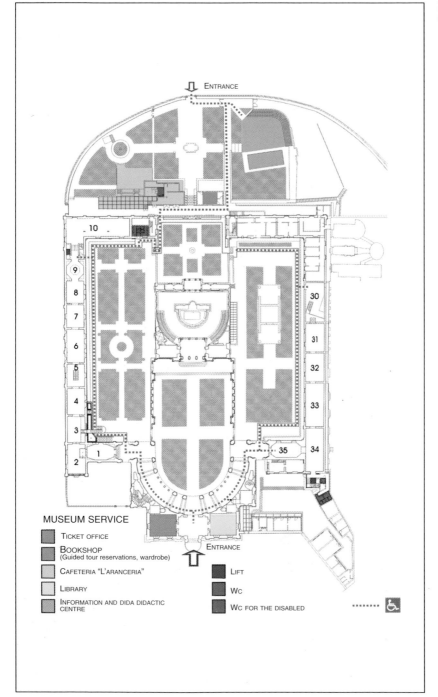

ENTRANCE

10

9
8
7
6
5
4
3
2
1

30
31
32
33
35  34

ENTRANCE

## MUSEUM SERVICE

TICKET OFFICE

BOOKSHOP
(Guided tour reservations, wardrobe)

CAFETERIA "L'ARANCERIA"

LIBRARY

INFORMATION AND DIDA DIDACTIC
CENTRE

LIFT

WC

WC FOR THE DISABLED

Plate II. Visiting the museum. Ground floor.

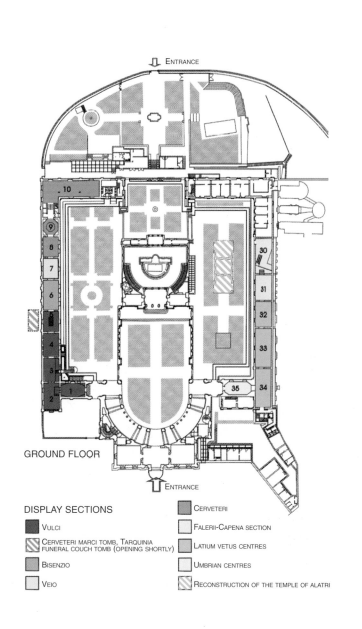

ENTRANCE

GROUND FLOOR

ENTRANCE

DISPLAY SECTIONS

VULCI

CERVETERI MARCI TOMB, TARQUINIA FUNERAL COUCH TOMB (OPENING SHORTLY)

BISENZIO

VEIO

CERVETERI

FALERII-CAPENA SECTION

LATIUM VETUS CENTRES

UMBRIAN CENTRES

RECONSTRUCTION OF THE TEMPLE OF ALATRI

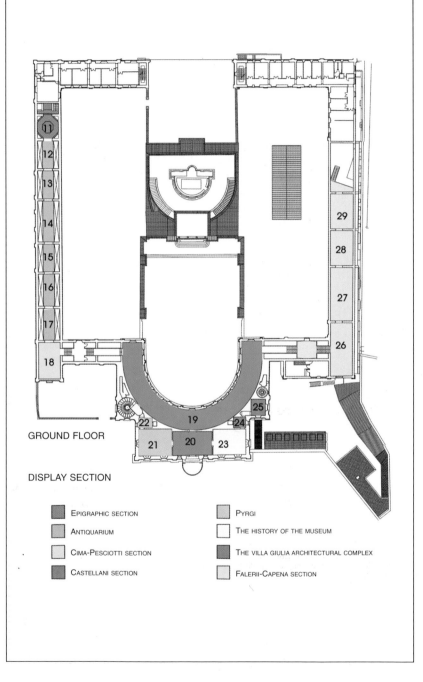

Plate III. Visiting the museum. First floor.

GROUND FLOOR

DISPLAY SECTION

Epigraphic section

Antiquarium

Cima-Pesciotti section

Castellani section

Pyrgi

The history of the museum

The villa giulia architectural complex

Falerii-Capena section

8

Plate IV. The
underground
areas of the Villa.

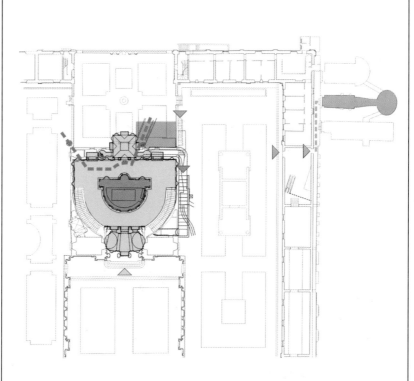

## THE UNDERGROUND AREAS
## OF THE VILLA

- ICEHOUSE (NEVIERA??)
- NYMPHAEUM FIRST LEVEL
- NYMPHAEUM SECOND LEVEL
- "VERGINE" ACQUEDUCT

- FROM THE GARDEN TO THE ICEHOUSE
- FROM THE LOGGIA TO THE FIRST LEVEL
- FROM THE GARDEN TO THE FIRST AND SECOND LEVEL
- FROM THE GARDEN TO THE "VERGINE" AQUEDUCT

Visits to the Neviera (Icehouse), second level of the
Nymphaeum and the "Vergine" aqueduct are to be
booked.

FAÇADE GEOMETRALE
DV PALAIS DV PAPE
IVLE, A ROME

# POPE JULIUS VILLA

Fig. 4. Villa Giulia. Façade of the "palazzo" in a watercolour design by an unknown French draughtsman in the late 17th century. (*Façade géométrale du Palais du Pape Jules 3 à Rome*).

Villa Giulia (*fig. 4*) was built according to the wishes of Giovanni Maria Ciocchi Del Monte, elected Pope with the name of Julius III (1550-1555), on a vast estate extending from land the family had possessed since 1519 from Monte Valentino, now known as the Parioli hill, to the other side of the Tiber. The plans Pope Julius had made to enhance his Vineyard included organisation of the area around the Villa with the extension of existing buildings and the construction of new features – fountains, pergolas, loggias and aviaries – which would represent so many visual reference points while also elegantly furnishing the vast complex. Further evidence of Pope Julius' intentions for his property can be gleaned from a letter written to Vasari in 1548, where he refers to large-scale works at Monte Sansavino to create the "*Georgica*", a villa to be built as part of his plans to extend and enhance his native town. The property was to be divided into two parts: the owner's villa, serving for his personal pleasure, and – separated by an avenue – the productive part. These features

recur in Villa Giulia, access to which was achieved with the construction of a road connecting the Via Flaminia to the Tiber to form what is now Via di Villa Giulia. The road was laid along the course of the old Arco Oscuro pathway leading to the vineyards on the slopes of Monte Valentino facing Villa Giulia and the road that led to Villa Poggio, the present-day Villa Balestra (*fig. 5*). The orientation of the villa was dictated by the particular lie of the land, the building being hugged between two tufa hills in a long, narrow valley.

Julius III's Villa derives from re-elaboration of an approach to composition that saw architecture taking on increasingly complex forms around the mid-15th century. This approach showed a new interest in associating figurative decoration, the use of materials and the expressive potential afforded by the theme of water, which underlies the organisation of the Villa itself. In fact, the architectural elements were organised along an axis following the longitudinal axis of the valley itself, which had the

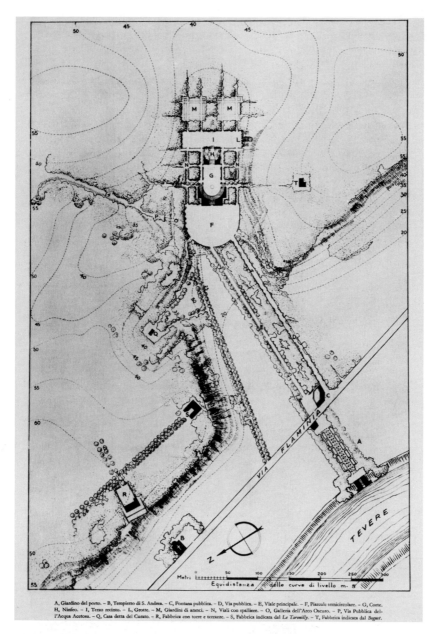

Fig. 5. Villa Giulia
in its original
setting (by M.
Bafile, *Villa
Giulia.
L'architettura, il
giardino*, Rome
1948 Poliservizi X).

A, Giardino del porto. – B, Tempietto di S. Andrea. – C, Fontana pubblica. – D, Via pubblica. – E, Viale principale. – F, Piazzale semicircolare. – G, Corte. H, Ninfeo. – I, Terzo recinto. – L, Grotte. – M, Giardini di aranci. – N, Viali con spalliere. – O, Galleria dell'Arco Oscuro. – P, Via Pubblica dell'Acqua Acetosa. – Q, Casa detta del Curato. – R, Fabbrica con torre e terrazze. – S, Fabbrica indicata dal *La Tarouilly*. – T, Fabbrica indicata dal *Bogaet*.

*Vergine* Aqueduct canalised in its
deepest part and at the other
end opened up on the broader
reaches of the Tiber basin.

Along this axis we encounter,
in sequence from the rear part
of the valley towards the Tiber,
the second courtyard, called the

12

Loggetta, the Nymphaeum with the sunken fountain (*fig. 6*), Ammanati's Loggia, the first courtyard and the Palace. Attribution of the general plan for the Villa is by no means a simple matter, although Vasari stated quite explicitly that he had been "*the first to design and realise the entire invention of the vigna Giulia*", subsequently including "*again in design the Pope's whims, which were then given to Michelangelo to revise and correct.*" He added furthermore that "*Jacopo Barozzi da Vignola with his designs finished the rooms, halls and many other ornaments of that place*", and that the sunken fountain was designed by himself and Ammannati, "*who then stayed and created the loggia, which is above the fountain.*" Nevertheless, it has recently been hypothesised that the original design of the villa complex was in fact by Vignola. As for the decorative elements, the general scheme is undoubtedly attributable to Ammannati, who personally moulded the stucco-work and sculpted a great many statues including the caryatids on the Loggia, and to Vasari, both helped by other artists including Pietro Venale da Imola for the decoration of the vault in the semicircular gallery (*fig. 7*). Decoration of the upper rooms (Halls of Venus or the Seasons, of the Seven Hills and of the Arts and Sciences) is attributed to Prospero Fontana, and of the ground floor to Taddeo Zuccari.

Fig. 6. Villa Giulia. The Nymphaeum: detail of the sunken fountain.

13

Thus the present state of the Villa is the outcome of numerous transformations, while organisation of the architecture along the longitudinal axis of the valley remains the constant factor. Indeed, many changes were made in the course of construction *"as new whims came to that Pope"* (Vasari): on the facade of the Villa (the Palazzo) we can see traces of a mezzanine window above the second window from the left, while other variants during the building work, detected in the course of the recent restoration, were made to the central part of the facade. The walls of the second Loggia wings facing the last courtyard still show clearly the remains of the octagonal pavilions which housed the two spiral staircases leading down to the Nymphaeum, closed while building was still underway and (what was left of them) brought to light during the conservation work of 1936. The late 18th century saw restoration work and Ammannati's Loggia was modified with the creation of two side portals opening onto the second courtyard. In the early 19th century the ramp leading down to the sunken fountain was built for the watering of the horses of the Veterinary School housed in the Villa. More recently, large-scale modifications were made to the Villa when it became state property, including windows opening in the walls of the semicircular gallery and, above all, the two outer wings created

Fig. 7. Villa Giulia. The semicircular gallery: detail of the vault decoration.

Fig. 8. Villa Giulia. The "Neviera" (Icehouse).

for museum and office space in the first two decades of the 20<sup>th</sup> century. This latter modification separated the organic architectural complex of the Villa from access to the Grottoes which Julius III commissioned from Vignola, who had them excavated and decorated with stuccoes and grotesques according to his own design (*fig. 8*). Notable, too, were the changes brought about by erratic attention to the conservation of the entire architectural complex, although most of the original features remain. We still have the various architectural components, the stuccoes and the decoration of the semicircular gallery and Nymphaeum, with the marbles and stones used to create them. However, only by comparing what we now see with the description Ammannati left of the Villa and its earliest iconography (*fig. 9*) can we realise just how much has been irremediably lost of the splendid polychromatic effects

15

obtained with coloured marble (still visible in the Loggia, by the hand of Ammannati, and in the sunken fountain of the Nymphaeum), a profusion of stucco and imitation marble (note the imitation marble left in the panels of the arch intrados on the facade, the exquisite stuccoes in the first courtyard and the ghosted imitation marble still glimmering in the panels), the partially restored stucco metopes of the Doric frieze in the Nymphaeum, and a wealth of frescoed surfaces now totally lost (note the sinopias in the two panels in the central part of the semicircular gallery and on the walls of the atrium), records of which are now only to be found in old engravings.

/tc/

Fig. 9. Villa Giulia. Elevation of the Nymphaeum. Detail from a watercolour design by an unknown French draughtsman in the late 17th century (*Coupe géométrale prise aplombs sur la ligne face du Palais du Pape Jules trois fabriqué proche de la Voye Flaminie à Rome*).

16

# ORIGINS AND DEVELOPMENT
## OF THE MUSEUM

The Villa Giulia Museum owes its origins to the late 1880s and a plan by Felice Barnabei (1842-1922) based on a systematic series of archaeological investigations. The aim was to reconstruct and illustrate the profile of a region on the basis of the findings obtained with co-ordinated topographic researches and targeted excavations. Thus survey, excavation, study and display of the finds were the distinct but closely correlated stages of a single project for archaeological protection and enhancement, for the first time in Italy extending to an entire district. The project was also to serve as a model for other ventures of the kind, and to offer public opinion – in Italy and abroad – evidence of the capacity acquired by the new administration of antiquities, instituted in 1875, to launch and carry out projects. The original core of the new museum's collections consisted of a set of material found at Falerii (now Civita Castellana), the capital of the Falisci – a population settled in the area delimited by the Cimini hills and the Tiber, where careful topographical survey was carried out in the 1880s. As the finds had to be sorted out and displayed they were provisionally housed in Villa Giulia – the fine Renaissance complex created near the via Flaminia in the mid-16$^{th}$ century by Pope Julius II – in the two rooms on either side of the entrance vestibule and in three rooms on the first floor rescued from the squalor of years during which the villa had been used for quartering and storage. The first exhibition (carried out in 1888-1890) and Barnabei's whole ambitious project received official sanction with the institution of the Museo Nazionale Romano (February 1889). Although conceived as a single unit, the new institution was divided into two sections – "urban" and "extra-urban" – according to the provenance of the material to be displayed. The first section was housed in the monumental premises annexed to the Baths of Diocletion, while the second remained in Villa Giulia, with the plan to bring together there all the objects found in the Roman province, including the part of Etruria coming within

17

the Rome region, the Faliscan Ager and Ager Capenas, the Sabine hills and Southern Latium. Thus the antiquities of *Falerii* saw the gradual addition of objects from other centres in the region (Corchiano, Narce, etc.) as well as finds from the built-up areas, sanctuaries and necropoleis of Southern Latium (*Gabii*, Alatri, *Satricum*, Colli Albani and, later, Palestrina), Etruria (Cerveteri, in particular the sarcophagus of the "Bride and bridegroom", and in due time Veii) and Umbria (Todi, Terni). According to the original plans, for various reasons never fully carried out, this material was to provide the first core of other collections which were to afford an overall picture of all the civilisations that had flourished in Latium and the neighbouring regions before the Roman conquest.

While the original collections have largely been conserved, changes in local jurisdictions and the great excavations carried out in the first half of the 20th century – in particular in Veii and Cerveteri – have had considerable influence on the character of the museum, accentuating the Etruscan strain. With the addition of two new wings symmetrically arranged to enclose the Renaissance courtyard with Loggia and Nymphaeum, the Villa Giulia Museum had by the '30s acquired the general appearance that was to remain much the same until the post-war period (*figs. 10-11*). Lack of room and new display criteria led to radical restructure of the museum on a plan by Franco Minissi, carried out between 1950 and 1975 by Renato Bartoccini, and

Fig. 10. The Museum in the 1930s. Room VII in the north wing, dedicated to antiquities from Vulci.

Fig. 11. The Museum in the 1930s. Room XII on the ground floor (now room 1), dedicated to the architectural terracottas and sculptures from the Portonaccio sanctuary at Veii.

subsequently by Mario Moretti. Thanks to Mario Moretti's initiative this period and the following years also saw the creation of a series of museums distributed over Southern Etruria to complement Villa Giulia and complete the general picture delineated there.

*[fd]*

# VULCI

Vulci (Etr. *Velc-*, Gr. *Olkion*, Lat. *Vulci*) rose on a plateau lapped by the river Fiora – the ancient Armine – at about 12 km from the sea. Although the sources offer scant reference, the importance of the city is attested by the extraordinary material turned up with excavations carried out here since the 18th century. As early as the 9th century BC the centre was evidently open to exchange and trading relations, which gradually increased as from the 8th and 7th century BC, when Vulci entered a period of grandeur that lasted through the 6th and into the 5th century BC. The city became an important nerve-centre for trade involving the major markets of the Mediterranean and extending through internal Etruria and the Po regions as far as the north of the peninsula, covering a vast area dotted with minor centres. Subsequent to economic recession hitting the centres of maritime Etruria as from the 5th century BC, the 4th century saw the city flourishing with renewed splendour. After the Roman conquest, in 280 BC, the history of Vulci was much like that of the other centres. Indeed, the city enjoyed a very long life, to become a bishopric in the 8th century AD.

## Room 1
Here we find two celebrated funerary sculptures in local tufa (nenfro) found in the Poggio Maremma necropolis. The older of the two pieces, datable to the first decades of the 6th century BC, is of a *centaur* –a fantastic figure, part man part horse (*fig. 12*). The second piece, of about thirty years later, shows a youth riding a sea monster. Placed to adorn sepulchres, both are the work of local sculptors influenced by coeval work in Greece, Daedelic in the case of the centaur, Eastern Greek for the rider, but successfully forging their own compelling figurative style.

## Room 2
The earliest evidence of the Vulci necropoleis dates back to the Early Iron Age (9th-last decades of 8th century BC, according to the conventional chronology), marked by cremation rites with the ashes of the dead gathered in characteristic biconical *impasto* urns together with a few grave goods. The earliest compositions show a general uniformity in the various contexts, but as early as the latter 9th century we find a gradual differentiation in the funerary contexts, attesting to the progressive structuring of social communities. Significant in this respect is the tomb of nuraghic Bronzes, which was of a lady of rank (latter 9th century BC) and yielded together with fine personal ornaments three small bronze objects

20

Fig. 12. Poggio Maremma necropolis. Funerary sculpture of a centaur in nenfro. Early decades of 6<sup>th</sup> century BC.

21

Fig. 13. Vulci, Osteria necropolis. Hut-shaped urn in bronze. Late 9th-early 8th century BC.

documenting early trading relations with Sardinia. Also attributable to eminent personages are the *biconical urns in bronze*, while the *hut urns* typical of the Latium area and modelled on real dwellings are somewhat rarer. An example of exceptional technique and elaborate decoration can be seen in a bronze from the Osteria necropolis (late 9th-early 8th century), documenting the considerable technological quality achieved by Vulci's bronze-workers (*fig. 13*). The 8th century saw a substantial increase in exchange and trade relations, and the imported material now in circulation gave a new spur to local production while, at least in the field of ceramics, immigrant craftsmen from Eubea also boosted its development. At the same time a process of social organisation was now reaching completion which saw the rise of the great aristocracies that would dominate Etruria until the Archaic period.

In the Orientalizing period (late 8th-early 6th century BC), so defined on account of the massive inflow of goods from the major Mediterranean emporia to Etruria, the old cremation rite was gradually abandoned, the dead being buried first in graves (ditch inhumation), subsequently preference rapidly changing to chamber tombs of even monumental proportions. The same period saw change in the composition of the grave goods,

22

now consisting of a greater number of objects. Documenting the earliest Orientalizing phase in Vulci is the noble tomb of the Chariot, datable to 670 BC, which yielded an extraordinary array of finely embossed bronzes of local manufacture, outstanding among which is the chariot itself (*fig. 14*), together with three small imported vases and a fine *impasto* set of local production. Dating to about forty years later is the so-called Constructed tomb in the Polledrara necropolis, which yielded a wealth of grave goods attributable to various generations of the same family including vases of Late Protocorinthian, Transitional, Corinthian, Eastern Greek and Phoenician (?) manufacture associated with a selected set of objects of local production. Outstanding among the material imported from Eastern Greece in the grave goods of chamber A, tomb 1/1986 in the

Cuccumelletta tumulus dating the last 25 years of the 7<sup>th</sup> century BC, is a rare kalyx from Chios (*fig. 15*).

## Room 3

Dating somewhere between 620 and 580 BC, the grave goods from the *Tomb of the Painter of the Bearded Sphinx* includes vessels imported from Corinth and Eastern Greece associated with Etruscan-Corinthian ceramics attributable to the major Vulci workshops of the period, bucchero (the fine black pottery of the Etruscans) vessels both plain and incised, and various objects in alabaster imitating imported types. Similar taste is shown in the choice of grave goods in *tomb 168*, Hercle excavations (last quarter of 7<sup>th</sup> century – second quarter of 6<sup>th</sup> century), where, together with a dish of Rhodes manufacture we find a silver-surfaced vessel imitating exotic oenochoai (wine-jugs) with ostrich egg shaped

Fig. 14. Vulci, Osteria necropolis, tomb of the Chariot. Chariot dashboard in embossed bronze. Between 680 and 670 BC.

Fig. 15. Vulci, Cuccumelletta area, tomb 1/1986. Kalyx from Chios, last quarter of 7<sup>th</sup> century BC.

bodies, again produced at Vulci in the Orientalizing period. Throughout the Archaic period Vulci flourished as ever, but gradual change came about in tastes and trade, with increasing emphasis on ceramics imported from Attica to the extent that, by the end of the 6<sup>th</sup> century, they were actually monopolising the Etruscan market. Local production adapted to the new models, owing part of its success to immigrant craftsmen from Ionia. Vulci's cultural horizon in the final decades of the 6<sup>th</sup> century BC is represented by the grave goods from tomb 177 of the Osteria necropolis which yielded, together with imported vessels and bucchero and bronze receptacles, a fine set of vessels in the Pontic style (*fig. 16*). From just a few decades later are the grave goods from tomb 145 at the Osteria necropolis, Hercle Exavations, consisting of bronzes and vessels imported from Eastern Greece and Attica including an outstanding kyathos

Fig. 16. Vulci. Osteria necropolis, tomb 177. "Pontic" kalyx. Around 520 BC.

Fig. 17. Vulci. Osteria necropolis, tomb 145. Black-figure Attic kyathos from Lydos. Between 560 and 540 BC.

24

from Lydos (*fig. 17*) displaying Dionysiac figures. Quality ware does not appear to have been limited to Vulci, but also found its way to various centres in the area. From Monte Aùto come grave goods including, among other objects, a fine *blue glass armilla* (armlet) with gold decoration, restored in ancient times (510 BC).

## Room 4
The fashions and customs in vogue in late 6th-century BC Vulci society are represented by *tomb 47*, Mengarelli excavations, found intact in the Osteria necropolis. Apart from a bronze trophy which evidently belonged to a hoplite – representing an emerging class in Etruscan society of the period – the grave goods consist of a sumptuous set of bronze banquet vessels together with bucchero ware and Attic black-figure material including a Panathenaic amphora with a boxing scene extolling the athletic prowess of the ancient warrior. Other funerary contexts attributable to the closing decades of the 6th century BC, mostly from the Osteria

Fig. 18. Vulci. Osteria necropolis, Mengarelli excavations, tomb 50. Black-figure Attic hydria by the Lysippides Painter. Last quarter of 6th century BC.

25

necropolis, include notably the *fondo Radicetti/1973 tomb*, which yielded not only a number of fine Attic vessels, including two "bilingual" (i.e. depicted with two different techniques) kylikes, and various bucchero, impasto and bronze pieces, but also a set of black-figure Etruscan vessels by the Micali Painter and his apprentices. From the same period we also have tomb 50, Mengarelli excavations, including a hydria by the Lysippides Painter (*fig. 18*) and a kylix with warrior heads by the Painter of Vulci, and *tomb 56*, with a kylix from Euaion. Finally, we have the somewhat exceptional *tomb 51*, datable to the early 4th century BC, which includes among the grave goods an earlier black-figure Attic amphora signed by Nikosthenes. Importation from Attica ceased between the Classical period and early Hellenism, and the market was dominated by local production. Far from the splendour of the previous centuries, the grave goods (*tombs 25, 52, 53, 54, 17, 19, 20*) now show undistinguished quality.

## Room 5

The sustained vitality of the Vulci sculptors' workshops in the Hellenistic period is attested by the *Guglielmi Altar*, the finely wrought *figured capital* and the monumental *sarcophagus* with scenes of Amazonomachy, discovered with just a few other objects in the tomb of Inscriptions found already desecrated in the Ponte Rotto necropolis. Displayed here along with a number of terracotta architectural elements are various votive offerings made to the divinities of health and fertility (votive offerings from Vulci-Porta Nord, Carraccio dell'Osteria, Legnisina and Tessennano Fontanile). In the form of divinities, seated or swaddled infants, parts of the human body, models of buildings, etc., these votive offerings are typical of central Italic production, giving genuine expression to a religious spirit common above all among the middle-to-lower classes.

*/amms/*

The ramp in the centre of the room leads down to the *tomb of the Maroi tumulus*, datable to the first half of the 6th century BC, here also exemplifying 1950s-style museum display of a funerary complex in the same conditions in which it was found. In an area immediately adjacent plans are underway to display the *tomb of the Funeral Couch* from Tarquinia, datable to 460 BC. The paintings removed from the tomb in the 1950s in the interests of conservation are among the most significant examples of the culture that flourished in Tarquinia. This Etruscan metropolis is not represented in the Villa Giulia Museum, but ample documentation is to be seen in the Palazzo Vitelleschi National Museum in the town of Tarquinia itself.

*[amms]*

Bisenzio (Lt. *Visentium*) was an important settlement rising on the west bank of the lake of Bolsena, dating back to protohistoric times. Subsequently it became an Etruscan centre, Roman municpium and Medieval village, declining in the late Renaissance and finally abandoned in the 18th century. The ancient built-up area presumably developed on Monte Bisenzio and its slopes, as recent research would appear to confirm. Investigation of the extensive Villanovan and Etruscan burial grounds stretching out round the settlement began in the late 19th century, since when it has brought to light a great many tombs with rich grave goods, well exemplifying the peculiar production of southern Etruria and attesting to relations with other centres, and with Vulci in particular. One of the most representative forms in Bisenzio's late-geometric vessel production is the footed earthen jar as represented by the example from Olmo Bello tomb 24 – a male burial attributable to the closing decades of the 8th century BC, with designs that seem to evoke the lake environment. The close links between Bisenzio and the

Fig. 19. Bisenzio, Olmo Bello necropolis, tomb 2. Bronze trolley. Last decades of 8th century BC.

27

Fig. 20. Bisenzio, Olmo Bello necropolis, tomb 2, pair of fibulae in gold, amber and bronze. Last decades of 8th century BC.

coast are evidenced not only by the ceramic products, but above all by the bronzes, including the famous trolley (*fig. 19*) from Olmo Bello *tomb 2* (burial in wood casket), which may have served as a censer or offering-trolley. Its rich sculptural decoration symbolically evokes the social structure of the emerging Etruscan aristocracy in its various activities – war, hunting and farming. The grave goods were evidently assembled for a woman, and included a gold necklace and a pair of fibulae in amber and gold (*fig. 20*). The same expressive vitality evidenced in the trolley can be seen in the situla from Olmo Bello tomb 22, attributable to the same chronological and cultural horizon. The situla is decorated with scenes of dancing around a chained animal (*fig. 21*). From Chiusi, and thus attesting to relations with northern Etruria, is the Canopic anthropomorphic cinerary urn yielded by *tomb 18*, whose grave goods are again datable around the late 8th and early 7th century BC.

Bisenzio continued to thrive throughout the 7th and 6th centuries, as is demonstrated by the quantity of grave goods (*tombs 68, 78, 84*). Among others, we may mention the grave goods from *tomb 80*, attributable to the latter half of the 6th century BC, including – along with black-figure Attic vessels and bronzes for

28

Fig. 21. Bisenzio, Olmo Bello necropolis, tomb 22. Bronze situla with sculptural decoration. Last decades of 8th century BC.

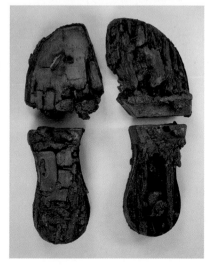

Fig. 22. Bisenzio, Olmo Bello necropolis, tomb 80. Sandals in wood and bronze. Latter half of 6th century BC.

banqueting – a pair of wood and bronze sandals (*fig. 22*) offering fascinating evidence of the uses and customs of the period.

As for various other minor centres of inland southern Etruria, the 5th century BC marked a phase of decline for Bisenzio, now cut off from the major traffic flows. This decline was to continue through the Roman conquest until the foundation of the municipium of *Visentium* in 90 BC.

29

Only 17 km from Rome and not far from the course of the Tiber, the city of *Veii* (Etr. *Vei(s)*, *Uentia*, Lat. *Veii*) rose on an extensive plateau delimited by the steep banks of two watercourses, the Valchetta (the Cremera River of ancient times) and the Mola waterway. In the area of fortifications at the southern end of the plateau stood the Citadel, with necropoleis containing thousands of sepulchres stretching out ring-wise around it. The classical sources record Veii as Rome's archenemy. The earliest clashes for control over the right bank of the Tiber, known as the "*ripa veiens*", date back to the times of Romulus, and the history of the city is marked by celebrated episodes of war including the defeat of the Fabii on the Cremera in 477 BC and, little more than thirty years later, the killing of Veii's King *Lars Tolumnius* by consul A. Cornelius Cossus in 434 BC. In 396 BC Veii was the first Etruscan city to be conquered by Rome, Furius Camillus successfully concluding a ten-year-long siege with mythical associations, modelled on the siege of Troy. Little of the extraordinary importance of Veii can be gathered from the evidence now displayed in the Museum, limited to the exceptional decorative cycle found in the Portonaccio sanctuary. Sacred to *Menerva* and various other divinities, possibly including Apollo, this place of worship standing by the city gates enjoyed fame far and wide, and was frequented at least as from the early 6th century BC. The various excavation campaigns carried out here have, in particular, brought to light an impressive temple, possibly dedicated to Apollo and Herakles (Hercules) to judge by their leading roles in the mythical episodes depicted on the coping. Built around 510 BC, it reveals in its layout the earliest known example of Etruscan-Italic buildings approaching Vitruvius' Tuscan model. Extraordinary here is the decorative display consisting of a complex of terracottas originally covering the wooden parts of the superstructure and, above all, the many larger than life-size statues that adorned the roof-top, mounted along the ridge beam on sturdy bases. Outstanding among them is the group of *Apollo (fig. 23) and Herakles* contending face to face over the golden-horned Hind of Ceryneia. Along with the two protagonists of the episode, which concluded one of the hero's twelve labours, there were *Hermes*, whose splendid head remains (*fig. 24*), and *Latona* holding in her arms the little Apollo, who may be using his bow to drive the serpent Python from Delphi. Exceptional, too, is the series of hand-moulded *antefixes* (high on the left wall) that covered the ends of the pantiles on the long sides of the weathering, with heads of a Gorgon (*fig. 25*),

Fig. 23. Veii,
Portonaccio
sanctuary.
Acroterion statue
of Apollo. Late 6<sup>th</sup>
century BC.

Achelous, Maenad and Silenus gazing out from shell-style nimbuses. The complex decoartive scheme datable to the closing years of the 6th century BC is the work of a great master, and one of the most original in all Etruscan art. He may well have been the artist recorded in the sources as "Veii's expert in terracotta sculpture", called to Rome under the reign of Tarquin the Proud to create the impressive terracotta quadriga crowning the Capitoline Temple of Jupiter inaugurated in Rome in

Fig. 24. Veii, Portonaccio sanctuary. Head of Hermes. Late 6th century BC.

Fig. 25. Veii, Portonaccio sanctuary. Gorgon-head antefix. Late 6th century BC.

32

509 BC. The picture of Veii offered by the Museum at present is to be filled out in the near future, but in the meantime a visit can be recommended to the area of the sanctuary in a virtually unspoilt rural landscape sung by Propertius in celebrated verses (IV, 10, 27). Here visitors can admire the superstructure rising over the ancient remains of the temple thanks to an evocative device conjuring up the temple, between reality and abstraction, delineating the proportions of the monument and the significant features of the decorative architectural elements.

*//fb/*

## CERVETERI

Cerveteri (Etr. *Ceisra*, Gr. *Chaire*, *Agylla*, Lat. *Caere*) rose on an extensive tufa plateau delimited by two watercourses. The necropoleis were situated around the city, on the Banditaccia plateau to the north, Monte Abatone to the south and the Sorbo hill to the west. Etruscan Cerveteri had three ports, *Alsium* (Palo), *Punicum* (Santa Marinella) and *Pyrgi* (Santa Severa). In the Villanovan period (9ᵗʰ-8ᵗʰ century BC) Cerveteri must have been an agricultural centre while nevertheless maintaining relations not only with Latium in general but also with the Greek world.
The real fortunes of the city began in the 7ᵗʰ century when it became the major centre for Etruria's maritime trade and, thanks to the export of raw materials and its own products, could afford to import refined goods from the East (vessels in precious metals, jewellery, ivories) and Greece (decorated vessels, bronzes, etc.). These goods were subsequently placed in rich sepulchres, mostly of a particular architectural tumulus type, possibly based on models in the Near East.
By the 6ᵗʰ century the city had a population of 25,000 and must have been one of the most important in the Mediterranean area, maintaining close relations with the Greek world that eventually became preferential – above all in the latter half of the 6ᵗʰ century – with the Greek cities in Asia Minor. Indeed, fleeing Persian conquest many of the craftsmen from there set sail for the coasts of Etruria.
In the 7ᵗʰ century political power had remained in the hands of a few aristocratic families, but as early as the 6ᵗʰ century wealth was being distributed over broader sections of the population. One result was the rise of the middle classes, as attested by the uniform cube tombs where Attic vessels continued to be deposited, although fewer in number and decidedly inferior in quality, showing limited narrative

ambition. Thanks to the victory won by Etruscan and Carthaginian fleets over the Greeks of Phocea off the Corsican coast, at Alalia, in 540 BC, Cerveteri was able to keep control over the Tyrrhenian for at least a few more decades, but the Etruscan defeat at Cuma in 474 BC spelt a certain decline in the city's wealth. In 384 BC the Cerveteri coastlands, and above all the port of Pyrgi, were plundered by the Syracusans, but soon after the city's fortunes took a better turn. Relations with Rome were now close, and Cerveteri enjoyed *civitas sin suffragio* status (citizenship but without voting rights) until 273 BC when, rebelling against Rome, it lost both Roman citizenship and coastland dominion.

## Room 8
Here we have examples of the Villanovan period grave goods from the Sorbo and Cava Pozzolana necropoleis: in terms of funeral rites, the most striking feature is the early introduction of inhumation alongside cremation. Particularly interesting are the grave goods from *pit tomb 253*, dating to the second half of the 9th century, with a jug-shaped ossuary (urn for bones) and three small cooking pots decorated with the mesh motif, and from pit tomb 199, possibly dating back to the early 8th century, with biconical ossuary and bowl-shaped lid in bronze lamina displaying embossed bird protome decoration. The grave goods in

the *tombs* of the *Hut, Ship, Montetosto tumulus* and above all the Chamber of Andirons, displayed in the next room (10), convey some idea of the variety and indeed the purchasing power of the wealthy aristocratic classes that had formed in the early 7th century and, intent on social enhancement and ostentation of wealth, adopted lifestyles from the more highly cultured Greeks, including convivial gatherings for banqueting. They also sought out luxury items, possibly exotic (e.g. an *ostrich egg* in the Ship tomb) or in precious metal (e.g. the *gold fibulae* in the Ship tomb and the *gold plaquettes embossed* with oriental-style winged figures from the tomb of the Andirons) or ivory (e.g. the *lion with a human figure lying on its back*, of Syrian production, and female figures on *goblet stands* from the Montetosto tumulus).

## Room 10
Just how much wealth was attained by the powerful families of Caere around 630 BC can best be appreciated observing the grave goods in the *Chamber of Andirons*. Still inviolate on discovery, it housed extraordinary Corinthian vessels, perfume jars in the form of human figures – from Rhodes in ceramic, from the east in gold-plated black stone (*fig. 26*) – together with a wealth of bronze vessels including great cauldrons, and utensils to cook meat (andirons and spits), again attesting to aristocratic lifestyles. Wealth can be seen not only in

Fig. 26. Cerveteri, Banditaccia necropolis. Chamber of the Andirons. Perfume jar in the shape of a human figure, eastern production in gold-plated black stone. Early 7th century BC.

Fig. 27. Cerveteri. Olpe in bucchero showing, in relief, Jason and Medea, the Argonauts and Daedalus. Ca. 630 BC.

the imported vessels and luxury goods, but also in the local production showing the influence of oriental-type iconographies, in circulation at least until the end of the first quarter of the 6th century BC: note, for example, the famous *Lion sarcophagus*, decorated with majestic sitting lions, datable around 580 BC, from the Procoio di Ceri tomb, and the fine bucchero vessels produced locally (e.g. the vase in the form of helmeted head with inscription, the goblets with heads in relief and the two situlae with animal decoration from the tumulus of the Painted Animals).

From the mid-7th century, and possibly earlier, a complex process of adaptation to the more cultivated models of Greek society got underway, one phenomenon of extraordinary importance being the transmission, and adoption by the Etruscans, of Greek myths associated above all – at least in the early stages – with the great Homeric epic of the Trojan War, adventurous exploration by sea, both westward as for example in the exploits of Odysseus, and eastward in search of precious materials and objects, as in the sagas of the Argonauts and the Golden Fleece, or the extraordinary deeds of the hero par excellence, Herakles, or Hercules – all well represented in the vessels displayed in room 10. A notable example here is the *bucchero olpe* (pear-shaped jug) (*fig. 27*) depicting in relief Jason and Medea, the Argonauts

Fig. 28. Cerveteri, Banditaccia necropolis, tomb 1 on the via Diroccata. Cretan hydria showing the blinding of Polyphemus. Around 520 BC.

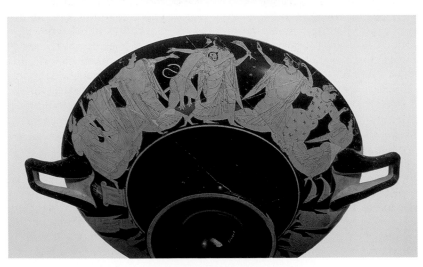

Fig. 29. Cerveteri, Monte Abatone necropolis, Martini Mariscotti tomb. Red-figure Attic bowl from Oltos. Ca. 520 BC.

36

and Daedalus – a veritable incunabulum of Greek myth in Etruria with personages unequivocally identified with their names in Etruscan, datable around 630 BC. Note, too, the *Caeretan hydria* from tomb 1 on the via Diroccata (*fig. 28*), showing Odysseus and his companions blinding Polyphemus in the course of their wanderings after the Trojan War, and the great *red-figure Attic goblet by Oltos* (*fig. 29*) dating to ca. 520 BC, with the deeds of Herakles (Nereus and the Nereids), from the Martini Marescotti tomb in the Monte Abatone necropolis.

The latter half of the 6th century BC saw strong artistic influence from the area of Eastern Greece that was to give rise the so-called Ionic current, superbly represented at Cerveteri by the famous *sarcophagus of the "Bride and bridegroom"*, displayed in room 9. Datable around 520 BC, it was to contain the ashes of the spouses portrayed here with a style characterised by elongated profiles, the archaic smile – not reflecting a state of mind but rather the attempt to create a sense of depth rather than flat features by drawing back the corners of the mouth – and the great pains taken over the folds in the robes and the hairstyle, all typical aspects of the figurative work in Eastern Greek art. Here, moreover, we also find a feature typical of peripheral cultures in the interest not so much in rendering the body as an organic whole as in emphasising the head and bust – the most distinctive parts of the human figure.

Probably directly attributable to the work of immigrant craftsmen are the *Caeretan hydriae*, produced at Cerveteri in very limited numbers and with just a few exceptions apparently never exported out of the city. They are decorated with lively scenes from mythology including the blinding of Polyphemus, mentioned above, the exploits of Herakles and the Rape of Europa, depicted on the hydriae displayed in the Castellani Collection, and Dionysiac scenes (grape-harvest, groups of satyrs and maenads) on a hydria from the above-mentioned tomb 1 on the via Diroccata. Another product of this cultural background is the famous *Ricci hydria* (*fig. 30*), with scenes of preparation for sacrifices on the shoulder and the apotheosis of Herakles, received on Olympus, on the body. However, as from the third quarter of the 6th century BC ceramic imports from Athens, both red-figure and black-figure, became preponderant. Given its purchasing power, the Etruscan market acquired some of the major masterpieces by the pottery decorators of the age: deposited in the *Martini Marescotti tomb* at Monte Abatone were the above-mentioned Oltos goblet with the deeds of Herakles and the amphora by the Painter of Priam, with the singular scene of ladies at the baths (*fig. 31*), while the famous *tomb of the*

37

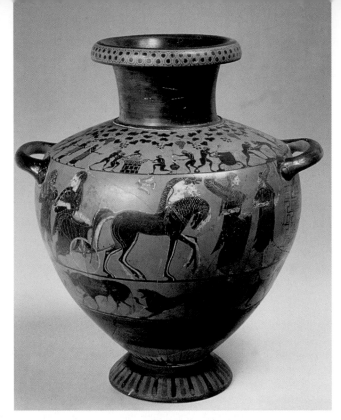

Fig. 30. Cerveteri. Black-figure hydria with a scene of preparation for the sacrifice on the shoulder and the apotheosis of Herakles on the body. 530-520 BC.

Fig. 31. Cerveteri, Monte Abatone necropolis, Martini Mariscotti tomb. Amphora by the Priam Painter with a scene of women bathing. Ca. 520 BC.

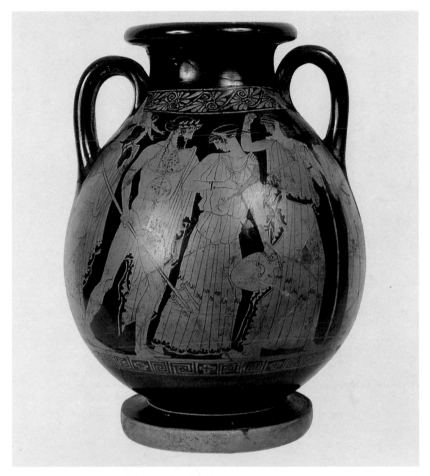

*Greek Vases*, used over a long period of time, yielded vessels almost exclusively imported from various workshops in the Greek world, particularly notable among which are some masterpieces from Hermonax (*fig. 32*). The Maroi tomb, in which a brazier was found containing remains of offerings including egg-shells, yielded various black-figure Attic vessels including, notably, a vase depicting Herakles fighting with a sea-monster, while a Banditaccia tomb contained the great *krater by the Berlin Painter*, datable around 480 BC. Also displayed are works of later production (4th-3rd century BC) including vessels from local workshops – Caeretan or Faliscan – with the typical cartouche oenochoai, and some vessels of fine quality such as the helmet-shaped vase.

39

*/mar/*

The Villa Giulia National Museum is one of the most prestigious museums dedicated to Etruscan civilisation, and when restructure was tackled along more rigorous lines fundamental importance was attributed to enhancing the collections with an epigraphic section, given the contribution language makes to our knowledge of this people's culture.

Hard a task as it is to sum up our present notions of the Etruscan language, the decision was made to bring to a larger public some idea of the gradual advances that have been and continue to be made in this field, while at the same time helping to dispel that aura of "mystery" that still wraps the Etruscan world to some extent, and in particular its language – a field that still sees "discoveries" as amazing as they are short-lived, based on etymological comparison with the most disparate languages.

To give an immediate idea of the overall state of affairs the epigraphic section is preceded by some words of a distinguished scholar, Massimo Pallottino: *"we are now able to understand the sense of the vast majority of Etruscan inscriptions, particularly in the case of the shorter texts......while at least the general sense can be grasped of even the longest and most complex of them."*

Of course, both light and shade emerge quite clearly as the inscriptions are illustrated, but the aim of the display is to stimulate the curiosity of visitors, and especially of the young people who will in the future be taking over the task of continuing research in an area that, given the steady spate of new finds, appears truly promising.

**Anteroom**

After the first panel with a brief outline of the history of studies on the Etruscan alphabet, its origins and the linguistic position of the Etruscan language, the display begins with presentation of some of the major texts including the Zagreb *liber linteus* (linen book), the longest text conserved, the Perugia cippus and the Laris Pulenas sarcophagus, which also illustrate the different types of inscriptions documented – religious, legal, funerary or associated with offerings. Among the more striking objects on display are the casts of the *Capua tegula*, the second longest Etruscan text we know, now conserved in the Berlin State Museums, and the *Pyrgi gold laminae*, two written in Etruscan, one in Phoenician, (*fig. 59a-c*) – the earliest epigraphic source for the history of Pre-Roman Italy. Among the noteworthy original pieces are the small bucchero perfume jar, the *aryballos Poupé* (*fig. 33*), adorned with a long and possibly amatory inscription on the shoulder, and the *Vulci olla*, undoubtedly manufactured on commission with rich decoration in relief framing the gift

40

Fig. 33. Cerveteri. Bucchero aryballos with a long inscription on the shoulder. Late 7th century BC.

inscription, also in relief. A map of Italy on the second panel illustrates the distribution of Etruscan inscriptions, showing that finds are mostly concentrated in the metropolises in Southern Etruria but fairly widespread in inland Northern Etruria.

## Room 11

The display cases on each of the walls are devoted to a particular aspect of Etruscan inscriptions. Thus, going clockwise, we find in the *first panel* information about the script and writing materials, known to us above all through depictions on figured monuments, such as the cinerary group from Chiusi with sculpted depiction of a textile book, consisting of a large rectangle of cloth folded over as the Zagreb *liber linteus* must originally have been. The glass case displays a cast of the *Marsiliana d'Albenga Tablet* showing along the margin a fine example of an alphabet table containing the 26 letters of the model Greek alphabet, and beside the tablet further examples of alphabet tables from various periods showing adjustments made to the alphabet to adapt it to the phonetic peculiarities of Etruscan. The second panel provides a commentary on the funerary inscriptions which, better than any others, show us the name designation system, the terms used for family relations and the way the age of the deceased was indicated. Note the inscription on the sarcophagus from Viterbo with the genealogy of Larθ Arinas and the inscription on the centre column of the tomb of the Claudi at Cerveteri, thanks to which we are now certain of the meaning of the words *apa* and *ati*, respectively "father" and "mother"; equally certain are the meanings of *clan*, *seχ* and *puia*, "son", "daughter" and "wife". The third panel deals with inscriptions of possession, from the earliest times of antiquity used to indicate the owner of a wide range of products. This particular category of inscriptions offers evidence of the meanings of a great many common words such as *śuθi*, "tomb", *mutna*, "sarcophagus" and the names of various types of vessels, some clearly being from the Historical Age borrowings from the Greek. Note the Archaic olla from Cerveteri where the vessel is defined *ϑina* from the Greek δῖνος, the *small jug from Veii*, called a *qutumuza* from the Greek κώτων (*fig. 34*).

Fig. 34. Veii. Impasto oinochoe with filter base and inscription. Second quarter of 7th century BC.

The *fourth panel* illustrates gift inscriptions that, in the Archaic period, attest to the custom of exchanging gifts among personages of rank, possibly even living in different centres, and the offering inscriptions which in later times usually record the divinity honoured and occasionally the reason for the offering. A fine gift can be seen in the gold fibula from Chiusi, with an inscription recording both possessor and donor. An inscription of dedication to the Dioscuri – a name translated literally into Etruscan as *tinascliniiaris*, "sons of Tina", the Etruscan Zeus – appears on the Attic kylix from Tarquinia. In the glass case are a small set of dedications from the Veii-Portonaccio Sanctuary, notable among which one on a goblet foot naming *Avile Vipiiennas* (*fig. 35*), much like the figure mentioned in the sources as Aulus Vibenna in the Roman saga of Servius Tullius.

The *fifth panel* shows inscriptions providing us with various names of magistrates and holders of priestly offices or representatives of the state, including coins and indications of city limits. The earliest mention of a public office, that of the *zilaϑ*, is on the Archaic funerary cippus from Rubiera (Reggio Emilia), while titles of the magistracy are recorded in the epitaph of Arnϑ Xurcles, whose was the sarcophagus from Norchia. A

Fig. 35. Veii, Portonaccio sanctuary. Bucchero vase with dedicatory inscription by Avile Vipiiennas. First half of 6th century BC.

particular case is to be seen in the wall inscription from Tarquinia, illustrated here on account of the interest of the two terms *capue* and *hanipaluscle*, referring to the city of Capua and to Hannibal, and thus to an event the man buried there had been involved in during the Second Punic War, between 216-211 BC.

Finally, the *sixth panel* is dedicated to the mythological and divine worlds which had such a part to play in Etruscan figurative art, and to the numerous caption-like inscriptions accompanying figures of gods and heroes, associated with forms of worship. There are many names – some of divinities, mostly of mythological personages – transliterated into Etruscan from the Greek and thus, through study of the adaptations, giving a very good idea of Etruscan phonemics. The earliest indisputable – because captioned – depiction of Greek myth in Etruria is on the olpe from Cerveteri dating to 630-620 BC, decorated in relief with episodes from the saga of the Argonauts (*fig. 27*) and in particular the sorceress Medea (*Metaia*) rejuvenating Jason and Daedalus (*Taitale*), the architect par excellence, equipped with spreading wings. A group of five of the "Seven against Thebes" – Tydeus, Polyneices, Amphiaraus, Adrastus and Parthenopaeus – can be admired on the Stosch gem. In the glass case, note the *Piacenza Liver*, a bronze model of a sheep's liver used as a didactic or mnemonic support for a haruspex (soothsayer). The upper face is incised with the names of divinities in outlined spaces of various dimensions, apparently distributed in such a way as to reflect the sixteen regions the Etruscans divided the celestial vault into for the purpose of receiving omens; on the lower face are two lobes, the names of the sun (*usils*) and of the moon (*tivs*).

/mpa/

## ANTIQUARIUM                          Rooms 12-17

Unlike the topographic rooms, the Antiquarium rooms contain material devoid of context, illustrating certain aspects of artistic Etruscan-Italic craftsmanship. Most of the finds come from the Kircherian Museum collections. Founded by the Jesuit father Athanasius Kircher in 1651, at the height of the Baroque period, with both naturalist and esoteric intentions, the Museum was housed in the historic Palazzo of the Collegio Romano. Under the administration of Contuccio Contucci (1735-1765) it took a more archaeological turn, to become a meeting point for scholars of antiquity. After Italian unification the cultural policy of the new state favoured a more explicitly archaeological character for the museum. The wealth of naturalist exhibits was

43

removed from the Collegio Romano premises, and in 1876 the archaeological collections were divided among three different museums – the Prehistoric Museum, the Epigraphic Museum and the Italic Museum. However, the Italic Museum failed to materialise and after a complicated series of events the material earmarked for it, originating in part from the 18th-century collections, went to the Villa Giulia Museum in 1913.

The present display is an attempt to recompose the old collection, thus documenting the scientific criteria and taste inspiring museum organisation in the first half of the 19th century.

## Room 12
Pride of place in the Kircherian Museum went to the celebrated Cista Ficoroni, datable around 350-330 BC (*fig. 36*). Found at Palestrina possibly in 1738 (the exact date is uncertain), it was

Fig. 36. Antiquarium, formerly in the Kircherian Museum. Ficoroni cista. Ca. 350-330 BC.

passed on from F. de' Ficoroni to his friend Contucci, immediately attracting the interest of scholars with its elaborate incised decoration, possibly deriving from a Greek "cartoon", illustrating an episode in the saga of the Argonauts, namely the boxing challenge King Amycus threw out to Pollux so that the Argonauts might make use of the spring. Interest was also aroused by the Latin inscription on the lid, recording the name of the craftsman – *Novios Plautius* – and the client *Dindia Macolnia,* for whose daughter the cista was commissioned.

## Room 13
The large collection of *bronze figurines* here exemplifies one of the most widespread types of votive offerings in the Etruscan-Italic sanctuaries, even after Romanization. They depict the faithful (men and women in offering or praying attitudes), priests (the haruspices with their characteristic conical hats) and the divinities (in particular those associated with the protection of men at arms: Mars/*Laran* and *Menerva*). The care taken over manufacture varies greatly, ranging from real miniature sculptures - notably the celebrated *Arezzo ploughman* group (*fig. 37*), datable to the last decades of the 5th century BC – to extremely simplified forms (*fig. 38*), which might be cut out from metal laminae.

## Room 14
Here we find a wide range of *utensils* and *vessels* involved in banqueting, an event of fundamental importance in the ancient world. Noteworthy as

Fig. 37. Antiquarium, formerly in the Kircherian Museum. Ploughman votive group from Arezzo. Last decades of 5th century BC.

45

exemplification of a *banquet scene* is the group of embossed laminae showing the scene with guests reclining on cushions, lyre players and servants, datable to the early 5th century BC.

The large collection of bronze tableware vessels, mainly to serve wine – jugs (wheel oinochoai (*fig. 39*), spouted oinochoai, olpai) and ladles (kyathoi) – or to separate and filter it, with the great variety of forms it reveals and the careful crafting of the decorative elements including finely *moulded handles*, attests to the high level achieved in technology between the mid-6th and 4th century BC by the Etruscan workshops, especially at Vulci, whose refined products

Fig. 38. Antiquarium, formerly in the Kircherian Museum. Small, threadlike votive bronze of a haruspex. 3rd century BC.

Fig. 39. Antiquarium, formerly in the Kircherian Museum. "Rhodian" oinochoe in bronze. Early 6th century BC.

were exported throughout the Mediterranean area. Also associated with banqueting, as the tomb paintings show, are the *candelabra* surmounted by anthropomorphic friezes, dating to the 6th-5th century BC, and the *tymiatheria* with figured stem, used to burn aromatic substances.

## Room 15

Here we find a collection of toilet implements illustrating another important activity for free citizens. The interest taken by women in this field is attested by the large collection of *mirrors (fig. 40)* – indispensable components of their grave goods from the 6th to the 2nd century BC – which

Fig. 40. Antiquarium, formerly in the Kircherian Museum. Bronze mirror. Latter half of 4th century BC.

found their most elaborate forms in the 4th century with complex mythological scenes and ornate frames and plant motives, and the *cistae* used to hold the toilet articles. These containers characterise the grave goods of Palestrina's women as from the mid-4th century BC, often in association with the typically elongated mirrors, one of which bears the signature of the craftsman, *Vibius Pilipus*. Also associated with body care, and in particular gymnastics, are the *powder boxes* and strigils to scrape the skin clean, datable to the Hellenistic period, as illustrated by the Attic *kylix* displayed in the same case.

## Room 16

In the Kircher collections bronzes received greater attentions than ceramics. However, it is worth noting the *figured balm jars of Eastern-Greek production*, which found great favour in Etruria. The warrior-head, Achelous-head and female-bust models were probably made in Rhodes, and of Rhodian or Milesian production is also the large *dish* with concentric ibex and bird patterns datable around 630 BC. Notable, too, is the Attic *black-figure column-krater* showing a Dionysiac procession evocative of its function as a wine container at banquets (530-520 BC). The Etruscan workshops are exemplified by a set of bucchero ware, a large Etruscan-Corinthian bowl dating to the first half of the 6th century BC and a *phiale* for libations with brown glaze decoration of the late 4<sup>th</sup> century BC. Note, too, the interesting pair of "*fish plates*" of Campanian production (latter half of 4<sup>th</sup> century BC).

**Room 17**
This room houses significant examples of vessel production in Greece, Etruria and Magna Graecia, acquired by the Villa Giulia Museum at various times. Quite extraordinary is the so-called *Chigi olpe* (*fig. 41*) from

Fig. 41. Antiquarium, Veii, Monte Acuto tumulus, Chigi olpe, ca. 630 BC.

the Monte Acuto tumulus north-east of Veii. A masterpiece of Late Protocorinthian (ca. 630 BC), the vessel displays all the skill of the Corinthian craftsmen, creating a unique work for the "Etruscan Princes". Also from the Monte Acuto tumulus is the *small bucchero amphora* with two alphabet sequences incised on the handles, attesting to the fact that writing was the domain of the aristocratic class in the Orientalizing period. Note also the kylix with Herakles and the Amazons, attributed to the Arkesilas painter – the best known of the Laconic pottery painters – datable around the second quarter of the 6th century BC. Noteworthy among the Attic ceramics is the *large black-figure amphora* with depiction of an ox being led to the sacrifice, dating to the mid-6th century BC. The somewhat unusual scene illustrates an important moment in religious life, when an animal as useful as the ox was exceptionally immolated. Equally noteworthy are the two *pelikai* attributed to Euphronios – the celebrated Greek master whose work as a ceramist is also known to us – and decorated with scenes of the life of the young. A particular line in Attic production is represented by the pair of *white-base lekythoi* datable around the mid-5th century BC. Associated with the cult of the dead, these vessels were decorated with scenes of the funerary world and often used as sepulchre offerings. Attributable to the Late Classical Age is the *hydria of the Mikion Painter's circle*, illustrating the madness of Lycurgus amid maenads and crazed women slaying his family before Dionysius and Ariadne. Noteworthy among the production of Southern Italy is the fragment of a *hut-shaped krater* from Buccino with the signature of Paestan pottery-painter Assteas, attributable to the class of "Phlyax" vases decorated with scenes inspired by mythology. Datable to the mid-4th century BC, the krater shows a parody of the Rape of Cassandra performed by Ajax on inverts.

Finally, we come to a work of Apulian production, namely the situla with the myth of Pelops and Oenomaos (personages indicated with their respective names), datable to the 4th century BC. Here we see the palace of Oenomaos, who is seated on his throne, and Pelops (to the left, wearing boots and Phyrygian cap) arriving to win the king's daughter (Hippodamia, leaning against a column) by challenging him to a chariot race.

*/mph/*

Originally consisting of roughly seven hundred pieces, about thirty of which were purchased on the antique market in 1964, the collection is mainly of material from centres in Southern Etruria, covering a time span from the 8th to 4th-3rd century BC. The essential core of the collection, consisting of about a hundred items of great quality, joined the antique Collections of the Villa Giulia Etruscan Museum after long and complex negotiations concluded in 1972. Today it occupies a particularly important place in the rich section dedicated to the Collections, in the context of which it effectively illustrates the taste and criteria guiding the "minor" private collectors, who must have been greatly encouraged by the extraordinary resources available in the Viterbo region. Among the earliest material, datable to the latter half of the 8th century BC, pride of place goes to an outstanding set of bronzes including three biconical vessels, possibly made in Vulci or Tarquinia, a Vetulonian-type censer and a fine pair of bronze horse-bits with small stylised horse adornments (*fig. 42*). To the end of the same century are attributable two *Italo-geometric oinochoai*, one characterised by Euboean-Cycladic decorative design much like the pattern appearing on a fine krater with stirrup handles, the other of Protocorinthian-Cuman type.

The Etruria of the Orientalizing Age (late 8th-early 6th century BC) is represented by a number of fine ceramics, both imported

Fig. 42. Cima-Pesciotti Collection. Bronze horse bit, latter half of 8th century BC.

50

Fig. 43. Cima-
Pesciotti
Collection.
Oinochoe by the
Swallows Painter.
Last decades of
7th century.

(mainly from Corinth) and
locally produced. Outstanding
among the latter are two
*oinochoai by the Painter of the
Swallows*, an immigrant
Eastern-Greek artist active in
Vulci around 620 BC (*fig. 43*),
while the Greek imports
include two rare *faience vases*,
one being of particularly large
proportions. There is also a

rich collection of bucchero
ware including two oinochoai
with fine incised animal
friezes, manufactured in Vulci,
while the characteristic house-
shaped cinerary urn with
white-on-red painted
decoration was produced in
the Cerveteri area. The cultural
horizon of the Archaic Age
(early 6th-5th century BC) is

51

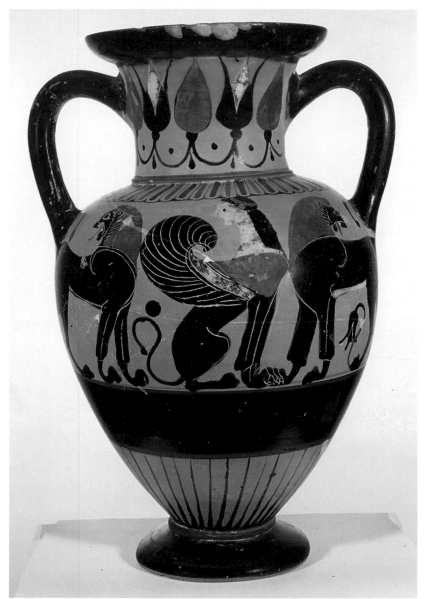

Fig. 44. Cima-Pesciotti Collection. Chalcidian-type amphora. Last quarter of 6$^{th}$ century BC.

well represented here with a Mesocorinthian *column-krater*, two *Chalcidian-type amphoras* (*fig. 44*), two *kalykes* belonging to the Vulci *Pontic Group* and a rare *Caeretan hydria* with a racing scene. There are also numerous Attic products from the Archaic and Late Archaic Age including a

Fig. 45. Cima-Pesciotti Collection. Black-figure Attic kylix of the lip-cup type, signed by Tleson. Ca, 540 BC.

pair of rare *type B panel amphoras* decorated with horse protome, a *goblet by Tleson (fig. 45)* and another by the potter Nikosthenes – all black-figure ware. Finally, Etruscan and Faliscan production of the 4th-3rd century is documented with two satyr-head antefixes and a number of characteristic red-figure vessels.

*[amms]*

## AUGUSTO CASTELLANI COLLECTION    **Rooms 19-20**

Here we have one of the most important collections of antiquities in the museum. Italian state property since 1919, it consists of over six thousand objects – as well as a great many fragmentary pieces, some of considerable quality – including ceramics, bronzes and metal artefacts, terracottas and items made of glass, ivory and bone. In addition we have ancient articles in gold along with the "modern" pieces produced over the years by the Castellani goldsmiths. The collection was assembled in the latter half of the 19th century – a time when intensive and indeed fruitful excavations were being carried out on the great sites of Etruria and Latium – thanks to the enthusiastic initiative of the family progenitor, Fortunato Pio. This friend and disciple of Michelangelo Caetani, Duke of Sermoneta, began to collect antiquities "*to replace in our city of Rome what the Pope sold to France in 1860*". The progenitor's work was subsequently carried on by two of his sons: Alessandro, an impetuous, romantic figure and a

53

Fig. 46. Inside the Castellani's "reception studio" in Piazza Fontana di Trevi in Rome: the room of modern jewellery (from C.G. Munn. Castellani and Giuliano. Revivalist Jewellery of the Nineteenth Century, Freiburg, 1984, fig. 15).

patriot eventually driven to exile, who continued his activities in the field of antiquities in Paris and, later, in Naples, and Augusto, the leading light. A central figure in the family history, Augusto gained a high reputation among the scholars of his time as a perceptive connoisseur of antiquities, and was also hailed as a patron of the arts and learning thanks to his handsome donations, enriching the public collections of the Capitoline Museums, where he was appointed honorary director in 1873. He was also director of the new Industrial Museum, which he himself had created in 1872. Expert in the goldsmith's art and a learned collector, he gave generous access to his famous collection evocatively displayed in the "reception studio" (*fig. 46*) at Piazza Fontana di Trevi and visited by the cream of European culture and aristocracy. After his

death it was his son, Alfredo, the last heir and champion of the family glories, who tenaciously strove through considerable difficulties to fulfil his father's intentions to leave the collection to the state, concluding the transfer in 1919.

The subsequent story of the Collection reflects the vicissitudes of the Villa Giulia Museum itself, where it found various forms of display over the years but remained substantially intact. Thus it still offers exceptional documentation not only of the tastes and fashions of 19th-century antiquarian archaeology, but also in its own right as material of extremely fine quality. After a long interval the Collection is on public display once again, arranged in such a way as to respect the original intentions of the owners to present the various classes of production in ordered succession. Within each class the

54

material is displayed on the basis of typological criteria taking due account of the chronological sequences and historical-artistic characteristics. Particular care has been taken over those rare groupings whose essential unity has been confirmed by the bibliographic and archive research carried out on the occasion of the present arrangement, and in display of the celebrated collection of jewellery in the central Room of the Seven Hills.

THE CERAMICS

**Room 19**
*North and central wing*

Assembled mainly between 1860 and 1870 with some particularly well-chosen purchases, notably of the rich *Caere* Calabresi Collection, this section assembles a wealth of material documenting the most important Mediterranean vessel production spanning a period from the 8th century BC to the Roman Age. Along with the earliest *impasto* and *red-on-white ceramic* exhibits, datable to the Orientalizing period (last quarter of the 8th century BC–first quarter of the 6th century BC), we find a series of *bucchero products* including the first from Etruria, whose production is attested in the 7th and 6th centuries. Well represented here is Corinthian production, including two olpai from the Chigi Group and a krater by the Louvre Painter, E 565, and *Etruscan-Corinthian* production including works by pottery painters such

Fig. 47. Castellani Collection. Volute krater of Laconic manufacture. 580-570 BC.

55

as the Castellani Painter and the Bearded Sphinx Painter. Then we come to the Eastern-Greek production, represented by a group of peculiarly shaped balm jars datable between the late 7th and early 6th century BC. Exceptional among the Greek Archaic period (early 6th–early 5th century) ceramics is the monumental *volute krater of Laconic manufacture* (580-570 BC) (*fig. 47*), together with which we may mention a rare Chalcidian psykter-amphora with

a painting of the judgement of Paris, and two Cearetan hydriae, the work of Eastern-Greek immigrants at the turn of the 6th century BC.

Ample room is dedicated to the black-figure Attic vases (ca. 560 BC-519/500 BC), including notably a hydria from Lydos with depiction of Herakles and Geryon (*fig. 48*), a fragmentary dinos by Exechias, a lip-cup by Tleson, two amphorae by Niksothenes and another by Antimenes, to name but a few celebrated examples.

Fig. 48. Castellani Collection. Black-figure Attic hydria from Lydos with Herakles and Geryon. 560-540 BC.

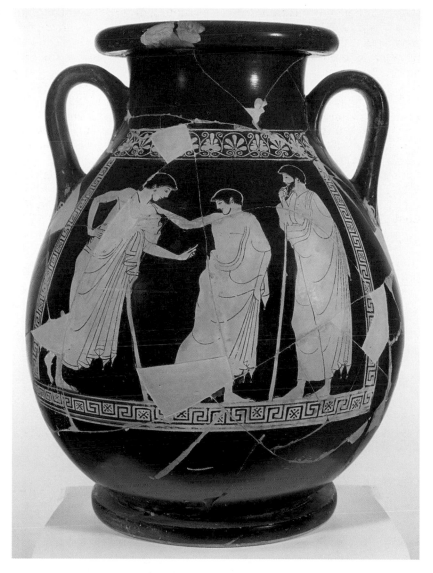

Equally fine in quality are the works of red-figure Attic production (520-440 BC), including a "bilingual" amphora by the Pamphaios Painter, a kylix by Oltos (*fig. 49*), two kalpides by the Kleophadres Painter (*fig. 50*), three vases by the Berlin Painter, a kylix by the Brygos Painter, a goblet by the Foundry Painter, a pelike by Hermonax, a kylix by Makron and, coming to the later production, works from the circle of the Pentesilea Painter, the Sabouroff Painter, etc. Here we also find Late-Classical and

Fig. 50. Castellani Collection. Attic red-figure kalpis by the Kleophrades Painter with Herakles and the Nemean lion. 490 BC.

Hellenistic production attributable to workshops in Etruria and Magna Graecia, including a number of *overpainted vases from Gnathia*, a lebès gamikós by the pottery painter Assteas, from the *Paestan workshop*, and a lekane by the Brunicki Painter, a product of the *Campanian workshop*. There are a great many *black glaze vases*, a number of silver-plated Late Etruscan vases and a group of *goblets from Megara*, datable to the Roman period.

THE BRONZES     **Room 19**
*South wing*

The collection of Castellani bronzes comprises about a thousand items. A wide range of production is represented here in terms of quality, forms and intended uses, largely attributable to Etruscan workshops and datable to a time span running from the 8th-7th century BC to the Late Roman. Thus, alongside a large collection of *banqueting vessels* of various forms and decoration we find material for *personal adornment* or connected with women's toiletry, as exemplified by the *Palestrina cistae*, including one complete with the articles it contained (*fig. 51*). However, various other contexts are also represented in the bronze

58

Fig. 51. Castellani
Collection. Cista
from Praeneste
(a) with contents
(b). First half of
3<sup>rd</sup> century BC.

section, including the princely
grave goods from the *Castellani
tomb* (first quarter of 7<sup>th</sup> century
BC). One of the most
celebrated of the Tyrrhenian
Orientalizing, the tomb was
discovered at Palestrina in 1861
and immediately joined the
Collection except for the
ceramics, which were probably
not collected at the time of the
excavation.
Subsequently the contents were
divided between the British
Museum and the Capitoline
Museums, only part remaining
in the property of Augusto and
eventually joining the other
material from the Collection in
the Villa Giulia Museum. Thus
we have the *bronze shields*
(*fig. 52*), the *bronze and silver
vessels* and a number of
*personal ornaments*. Particular

59

Fig. 52. Castellani Collection. Palestrina, Castellani tomb, bronze shield. First quarter of 7<sup>th</sup> century BC.

mention is merited by a number of other objects including a monumental *bronze kalyx with caryatids* (*fig. 53*) from *Caere* (last quarter of the 6<sup>th</sup> century BC), a group of rare "*lacunars*" (sunken ceiling panels) from Tarquinia (last quarter of the 7<sup>th</sup> century BC) and a sizeable collection of *Etruscan-Italic and Roman statuettes*, mostly representing divinities, to which we may add a small *Sub-Minoan bronze* of a female figure and the well-known statuette of Alexander as hunter (*fig. 54*), attributable to Greek production.

Fig. 53. Castellani Collection. Cerveteri. Bronze goblet with caryatids. Last quarter of 7<sup>th</sup> century BC.

60

Fig. 54. Castellani Collection. Statuette of Alexander as hunter. First half of 3<sup>rd</sup> century BC.

THE JEWELLERY                    **Room 20**

This is evidently the most spectacular part of the whole Collection. In the present display, which sees ancient and "modern" confronting one another, the idea was to restore this section to the special role ascribed to it in the original "Castellani studio" (*fig. 46*). Assembled in a relatively short space of time, the aim was to illustrate the history of the goldsmith's art with individual objects, preference going to Etruria, Magna Graecia and the Roman world. An impressive sequence of items is offered by the archaeological collection, which is arranged on a chronological basis while also taking account of the original contexts where possible, as in the case of the princely *Galeassi tomb* (early 7<sup>th</sup> century BC), discovered at Palestrina in 1861, for which we have the splendid *pectoral in gold and amber* (*fig. 55*) and three finely-wrought figured pendants in amber. Among the Archaic period (early 6<sup>th</sup>-early 5<sup>th</sup> century BC) jewels we may mention the fine set of *box-shaped earrings*, the *figured bow fibulae* and the *bezel rings*

61

decorated with stylised scenes. The magnificence of Late-Classical, Hellenistic, Etruscan and Magna Graecian production can be admired in the splendid *golden crowns*, the elaborate earrings showing the odd Baroque turn of taste, and again in the elegant *necklaces with pendants* (*fig. 56*). A more sober taste is revealed by the *Roman Age jewels*, some of which in silver, enhanced with resplendent chromatic effects; these are followed by a series of Late Ancient and Barbarian jewels, the stylised decoration often picked out with gems, coloured glass or semiprecious stones. Catellani's interest also went beyond the ancient, as attested by various pieces of the *Italian goldsmith's art* datable between the 13th and 19th centuries, a set of "*modern jewellery from the Abruzzo Apennines*" (Castellani

said it came from the booty of brigands), some isolated items from the *Far East* and, finally, a fine set of jewellery from the *New World*. The display closes with a section dedicated to glyptics (gem carving and engraving), with a selection of scarabs dating from the Classical to the Hellenistic period and including two rare objects from the Aegean world, namely an agate gem with the depiction of two genii, and a diadem made of fine plaquettes of glass paste of an intense blue, after the colour of lapis lazuli. Confronting the ancient jewellery, eight panels display Castellani's copies, variants and re-elaborations, to which are added the original creations of the workshop itself, showing a decidedly neoclassical taste. For the new display it was thought fitting to retain the original order,

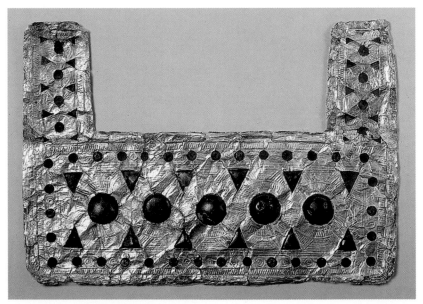

Fig. 55. Castellani Collection. From Palestrina, Galeassi tomb. Pectoral in gold plate and amber. Early 7th century BC.

Fig. 56. Castellani Collection. From Tarquinia. Necklace with miniature amphora pendants (Catsellani reconstruction from two necklaces of similar typology, style and chronology). 4<sup>th</sup> century BC.

Fig. 57. Castellani Collection. Castellani workshop, "Tyrrhenian Period". Pendant in the form of Achelous' head.

and thus the jewels are presented in the sequence Augusto attributed to them with the "*primordial*" followed by the "*Tyrrhenian*" (*fig. 57*), "*Etruscan*", "*Siculan*" (Sicilian), "*Roman*", "*Medieval*", "*Renaissance*" and, finally, "*modern*". As the eye scans these precious objects we can picture the extraordinary activity of the Castellani family – indeed, their jewels includes replicas of famous originals conserved not only in the archaeological section but also in various other famous collections in Italian and foreign museums. The copies may even introduce variations on the themes, often including incised gems (*fig. 58*),

63

cameos or scarabs, set using the "*oro giallone*" (dark yellow gold) that was one of the workshop's happy inventions. Frequent, too, are the *parures* reflecting the taste of the times. The backs are marked with a monogram consisting of two letter Cs intertwined: the hallmark of products in vogue among the great families of Europe.

A chapter apart would be merited by the *Castellani creations*, or the exquisite *micromosaics*, not to mention the array of objects crafted for the royal family and various other illustrious figures of the time. The Castellani family production came to an end in the closing decades of the 19th century, the neoclassical taste that constituted their essence also becoming a limitation. With the rise of *art nouveau* the workshop's creations appeared superseded, and decline soon set in.

/amms/

Fig. 58. Castellani Collection. Castellani workshop. Brooch with cameo in cordierite.

# THE *PYRGI* SANCTUARY

**Rooms 21-22**

Room 21, called the room of Venus, or of the Seasons, after the fine frescoes adorning it, and the adjacent room 22 house the important material from the sanctuary of *Pyrgi* (Gr. *Pyrgoi*, Lat. *Pyrgi*) – one of the ports of ancient *Caere* (see above) – brought back to light not far from the Castle of S. Severa, about 50 km north of Rome. The Greek and Latin sources offer numerous references to the sanctuary plundered by Dionysius of Syracusa, while systematic exploration of the complex was achieved in the course of over forty years of excavations carried out in the area by the University of Rome Department of Etruscan Studies.

The sanctuary rose to the south

Fig. 59 a-c. *Pyrgi* sanctuary. Gold laminae inscribed in Etruscan and Phoenician. Ca. 500 BC.

of the built-up area by the coastline, covering about six hectares. Delimited by a wall (*temenos*) opening on the north side to the major thoroughfare leading to *Caere*, it developed through a whole array of buildings in the course of time. In particular, at the end of the 6th century BC the king of *Caere, Thefarie Velianas,* launched a great building scheme that saw the sanctuary area taking on extraordinarily monumental features over the following fifty years. It was during this period that the first of the two temples ("Temple B") was raised on a huge earthwork in "area C", which was dedicated to the chthonian or underworld cult, as well as the long "Twenty cells" building, which came to abut on the long south side of the *temenos*. Associated with the foundation of temple B are the celebrated gold laminae bearing inscriptions (two in Etruscan and one in Phoenician) found in "area C", where they had been deposited in the 3$^{rd}$ century BC protected by material from the demolished temple B (*fig. 59a-c*). Two of these – one in Etruscan, one in Phoenician – record how *Thefarie Velianas*, king of *Caere*, dedicated a statue and a place of worship to a goddess called Astarte in the Phoenician text and *Uni* in the Etruscan. The third lamina, bearing a shorter inscription in Etruscan, records not only the institution of the cult but also the ritual performed.

**Room 21**
Along the wall to the left of the entrance are displayed various architectural elements from *temple B*, together reconstruction of the right *rampant pediment*. On the adjacent wall we see a selection of *antefixes* from the "Twenty cells" complex, which housed the priestesses consecrated to the goddess Astarte-*Uni*.
The building of *temple A*, reconstructed here with a *model*, around 460 BC marks the conclusion of the complex development plan launched at

Fig. 60. *Pyrgi* sanctuary. Temple A. Fronton high-relief with depiction of the Seven against Thebes myth. Ca. 460 BC.

Fig. 61. *Pyrgi* sanctuary. Temple A. Female head, possibly of *Thesan*-Leucotea. Datable between the second and third quarter of 4<sup>th</sup> century BC.

the end of the 6<sup>th</sup> century. The sanctuary area was now doubled in a northerly direction and a new earthwork raised for the erection of temple A – a grandiose project reflecting Caere's determination to reassert her maritime power after the defeat suffered by the Etruscans in the waters of Cuma in 474 BC.

The temple was dedicated to Leucotea-Ilizia, names that can again be identified with the Etruscan *Uni*, and has yielded some truly extraordinary

material. Pride of place here goes to the celebrated *high relief* originally adorning the rear side of the temple (*fig. 60*). Recently restored, the high relief illustrates one of the most dramatic episodes of the Seven against Thebes, the deadly duel between Tydeus and Melanippo observed in horror by Athena; appalled at the sacrilegious deed perpetrated by Tydeus, she takes back the immortality she had vouchsafed the hero, her sometime protégé. This first episode is accompanied by a second which sees *Zeus* springing at Capaneus in the place of Polyphon. Also featured in the display, together with two Caeretan-type *antefixes*, are two well-known sculptures from subsequent phases in the temple's building history, namely the *Herakles bibax* and the superb head of a woman (*fig. 61*), possibly *Thesan*-Leucotea, datable between the middle and the third quarter of the 4th century BC. Finally, from the southern area where excavation is now underway we have an *acroterion* depicting Achelous, the anthropomorphic bull.

**Room 22**
In the small adjacent room we find the *gold laminae bearing inscriptions (fig. 59a-c)* mentioned above and a *board of Syracusan coins*, possibly once part of the sanctuary treasure, and a votive dedication by *Tanachvil Carthereai to Thesan.*

/rc/

## THE HISTORY OF THE MUSEUM                    Room 23

At this point in our visit we come to a room (23) dedicated to the origins of the Villa Giulia Museum with particular reference to the happy and hapless vicissitudes behind the formation of the collections, as outlined in the introductory pages to the guide by Filippo Delfino (pp. 17-19). This is also an opportunity to present the protagonists of the story – major figures in Italian archaeology in the closing decades of the 19th century – while the panels displaying documents and period photographs reveal the radical changes the museum has gone through in its first hundred and ten years.
Further documentation of the museological and museographical approaches prevailing when the Villa Giulia Museum was founded is offered by the two 19th-century style display cases. Retrieved from the depots with the help of good luck, they show a selection of material from the Falsican ager belonging to the original core of the collections.
The prospects opening up with the forthcoming extension of the Museum are illustrated on panels to the right of the entrance, while the modern glass case by the windows in the facade looking on to villa Poniatowski will contain a series of displays showing the major additions to the collections, both recently discovered and purchased.

/amms/    68

With reorganisation of the rooms on the main floor a new section has been dedicated to the rich architectural complex housing the Etruscan Museum.

## Room 24

With the help of a model the early stages in the life of the complex are illustrated together with the transformations it has undergone over time, from the original purposes of leisure and relaxation to the various other uses. At one time serving as an official residence – accommodating among others Queen Christina of Sweden – the Villa has also housed a hospital, a veterinary school and military quarters, being used as a depot by the Engineers Corps. In 1889, not without difficulties, it became museum premises, housing the rich collections of Faliscan antiquities.
The large-scale model illustrates not only the extensions carried out in the early decades of the 20th century but also present developments. By including Villa Poniatowski with its roomy outbuildings, linked up with Villa Giulia by a pleasant avenue running below Villa Strohl-Fern, it shows the definitive organisation of Rome's Etruscan Museum Complex.

## Room 25

This room is dedicated to the 15th-century villa, outlined in its history and architectural conception by Tancredi Carunchio in the introductory pages to this guide (pp. 11-16). Pope Julius III's ambitious scheme and the exceptional results achieved, now more readily appreciated thanks to the restoration works carried out with Jubilee Year financing, are illustrated with a model, rare drawings (17th century) and a number of fine prints, all belonging to the museum's great patrimony, as indeed does the bust of Julius III to be seen in the corridor.

*/amms/*

## FALISCAN-CAPENAS SECTION          **Rooms 26-31**

This section is dedicated to two populations that although, as linguistic documentation attests, of different origins – the Faliscans Latin, the Capenans Sabine – shared the same tendency to gravitate towards the right bank of the Tiber and showed various cultural affinities. The Faliscan-Capenas collections were assembled between the closing decades of the 19th century and the early years of the 20th. Particularly outstanding are the Falsican antiquities, acquisition of which was closely bound up with the formation of the original core of the museum collections. Indeed, the Museum opened in 1889 to display the grave goods from Falerii – the major centre in the Faliscan area – being brought to light with the excavations of those years. The present display was arranged in 1998.

*Capena and the "minor" centres in the Faliscan ager:*
*Corchiano, Vignanello and Nepi.*

## Room 26

The Capenan communities settling along a fairly limited strip of land situated within a meander of the Tiber south of Monte Soratte centred on *Capena* (Gr. *Capínna*, Lat. *Capena*). Developing as from the 9th century BC on the Civitucola hillside, the ancient centre appears to have enjoyed considerable cultural independence from Etruria and the neighbouring Faliscan ager while showing affinities with Latium and the Sabine area. The centre saw its heydays between the late 8th and 7th centuries BC, when the "Orientalizing" phase was at its height and Capena became an important centre controlling the traffic along the Tiber valley, acquiring rare and precious items imported from the east. The iconographical motives displayed by these luxury goods offered models for the prolific but refined local production of

*impasto* ceramics crafted with incision and bas-relief techniques, alongside which flourished equally recherché bronze production. Some examples can be seen in the material displayed, including the *belt plates* with openwork decoration typical of female dress, the bronze *armour-disc* decoratively embossed with fantastic animals and the vessels found among the grave goods from *tomb CXIV* in the S. Martino necropolis, among the richest of Orientalizing Capena. After the Roman conquest (395 BC) Capena continued to enjoy urban life, albeit on a modest scale. Notable among the grave goods of this period are those from *tomb 233* (IV) in the necropolis delle Macchie, which include the famous plate displaying an elephant decked for war followed by a baby elephant (*fig. 62*). The plate belongs to a set probably created on the occasion of the victory of Curius Dentatus over king Pyrrhus of Epirus in 275 BC.

From this room we go on to documentation of the so-called "minor centres". The display of material from the Falsican ager follows a topographic sequence continuing up to room 31. The "minor centres" of the Faliscan ager, *Corchiano* and *Vignanello* (the ancient names are not known) to the north and *Nepi* (Etr. *Nepet*) to the south-west, offer the major evidence of a population distributed throughout the area, in these cases taking on real urban status as from the 7th BC. So much is attested by the

Fig. 62. Capena, necropolis "delle Macchie", tomb. 233 (IV). Plate with elephant decked for war. Second quarter of 3ʳᵈ century BC.

burials of the local aristocracy, including in their grave goods such outstanding items as the *clay stand* with diminutive horse and chain motives from Corchiano and the *alabastron* in Ionic bucchero from Vignanello, a rare example of Eastern-Greek ceramic imports in the Faliscan ager.

*Narce*

**Room 27**
Halfway along the river Treja, between Mazzano and Calacata, rose the most important centre in the southern Faliscan ager. We

do not know the ancient name of the city (identified by some as *Fescennium*) that developed on the three hills of Narce (hence the name attributed to the settlement), Monte Li Santi and Pizzo Piede, surrounded by a great many necropoleis excavated in the late 18th century and datable between the 8th and 3rd centuries BC. The site saw its most vigorous development between the late 8th and 7th centuries BC, when control over the major routes traversing the Tiber valley led to particularly early and significant contact with Greek culture. Valuable evidence

71

of this is offered by Petrina *tomb 4* (XXXIV), dating to 730-720 BC, where the cremated remains of a wealthy horseman were conserved. The ashes, cinerary urn in bronze lamina, ceremonial sword and phalerae of the horse-gear were protected with a cloth as in the Greek type of ritual described by Homer for the funeral of Patroclus. During the 7th century BC the local aristocracy achieved levels of opulence comparable with those of the "*principes*" of Etruria and Latium, as documented by the grave goods from the tombs "*of the Chariot*", "*the gold jewels*" and (*fig. 63*) and "*the shields*". In these burials the array of accompanying grave goods, including Faliscan *impasto*

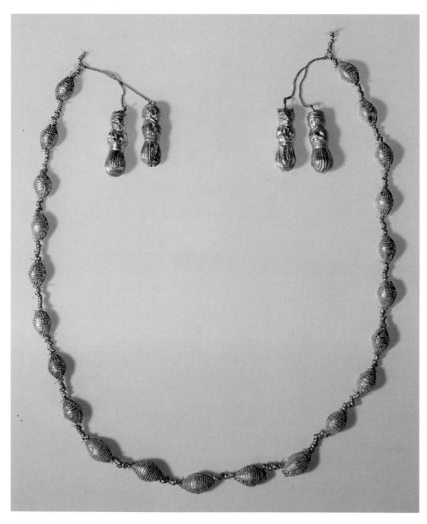

Fig. 63. Narce, Monte Cereto necropolis, tomb, 103 ("tomb of the gold ornaments"). Gold necklace. 7th century BC.

72

products, vessels cast in bronze and embossed, ceramics of Greek importation and from the Etruscan area would be enhanced with the display of precious personal goods stressing the status of the deceased, such as his chariot, ceremonial bronze shields, gold jewellery, silver and amber.

*Falerii*

**Room 28**
Capital of the Faliscan area, Falerii (Gr. Falérioi, Lat. Falerii) stood on the site of present-day Civita Castellana, on a high tufa plateau delimited by watercourses and endowed with natural defences. Development here began in the 8th century BC although there was some precedent in the Late Bronze Age (10th century BC), the ancient settlement extending over the plateau where the present town stands and over the contiguous Vignale heights. The evidence offered by the extensive necropoleis on the fringes of the built-up area and the many important urban and suburban sanctuaries pieces together a picture of great prosperity and thriving cultural activity until the Roman conquest in 241 BC. The greatest splendour was achieved in the 4th century BC when new urban and building development went hand in hand with a happy and creative season for the arts. Already engaged in the manufacture of architectural and votive terracotta and bronzes, *Falerii Veteres* now became an important centre for ceramics, largely for export (red-figure, overpainted and black glaze production) thanks to the immigrant Greek craftsmen. In more common and standardised forms this production continued into the following century. With the Roman conquest the city was razed to the ground (only the sanctuaries continued to be frequented) and ceased to exist, while the surviving population were moved a few kilometres away, and a new town arose on level ground with the name of *Falerii Novi*. This room contains evidence of the earliest funerary practices in the settlement, datable to the 8th and 7th centuries. Note in particular the grave goods from the pit and ditch tombs of the Montarano necropolis, the most archaic of *Falerii*'s burial grounds dating as early as the pre-urban phase. An interesting piece here is the house-shaped *cinerary urn* in bronze lamina (mid-7th century BC), the lid being a faithful reproduction of a roof with double weathering. Dating to the same period are the grave goods from *tomb 8* (XLVII) from Celle, one of the most extensive and important of the city's necropoleis: note the set of banquet ware (holmos, kantharos and amphora) in impasto with red on black decoration, probably of Falsican production. Finally, we have some important documentation of the Faliscan language attesting to the popularity of the cult of Dionysius among the city's aristocracy in the 7th century BC.

73

## Room 29

The economic and social rise of *Falerii* in the course of the 6th and 5th BC centuries until the city achieved its greatest splendour in the 4th century BC finds ample documentation both in the grave goods displayed in this room and in the temple architecture represented in the following rooms. The grave goods now include fine ceramics imported from Greece with real masterworks such as the *astragal-shaped vase from Syriskos*, the *vase in the shape of a dog's head by the Brygos Painter* (*fig. 64*), the *psykter from Onesimos* with the fight between Lapiths and the *stamnos by the Argo Painter* with Herakles and the centaur Pholos, from the first half of the 5th century BC. Alongside these fine works we find a masterpiece of the local artistic production, the monumental Aurora krater showing Eos (Aurora, goddess of dawn) and Kephalos on one side and Peleus and Thetis (father and mother of Achilles) on the other (middle decades of the 4th century BC).

## Room 30

Here, arranged to suggest the original architectural forms, are displayed pieces from the architectural facing of the *sanctuary of the "Sassi Caduti"*, sacred to Mercury (5th century BC–1st century AD). Remarkable here is the Late Archaic phase, well represented by the varied series of *antefixes* with Maenad-Silenus couples and the splendid *acroterium* with duellers,

Fig. 64. *Falerii*. Celle necropolis, tomb 16. Rython in the shape of a dog's head. Brygos Painter. First half of 5th century BC.

showing clear Greek and Magna-Graecian influences (*fig. 65*). The latest of *Falerii*'s sanctuaries – the *Scasato* sanctuary – was dedicated to Apollo and rose in the centre of the urban area between the late 4th and early 3rd centuries BC. World famous is

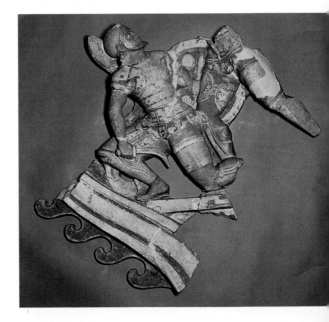

Fig. 65. *Falerii*, sanctuary of Mercury at "Sassi Caduti". Central acroterion with two duelling warriors between volutes. First half of 5th century BC.

Fig. 66. *Falerii.*
Scasato sanctuary
of Apollo.
Fronton statue of
Apollo. Late 4th-
early 3rd century
BC.

the series of statues from the fronton tympanum, while interpretation of the mythological picture they form is still a matter of debate; at the centre of the grouping we see Apollo (*fig. 66*) in his role as an oracular divinity. The sculptures by local terracotta artists reveal the

influence of the Greek stylistic canons in vogue in the Late Classical period, eclectically reworked.

**Room 31**
The fronton sculptures displayed here were found scouring the museum's

75

Fig. 67. *Falerii*, Scasato sanctuary of Minerva. Fronton high-relief depicting Juno. Early 4th century BC.

storehouses. They come from another important sanctuary, again rising in the *Scasato* area and dating to the 4th century BC, situated at the east end of the plateau and possibly dedicated to Minerva. Particularly fine quality is exhibited by the complex of high reliefs with statically posed figures – Minerva (*fig. 67*), Jupiter and Juno are clearly identifiable – showing quite distinctly the influence of Attic art as it was in the latter half of the 5th century BC.

Sacred to Apollo was the *sanctuary of the Vignale*

*acropolis* (5th-2nd century BC), which yielded a significant crop of votive offerings, the most interesting collection being mainly of fine quality heads and masks. Mentioned by Ovid in the *Amores* (*III*, 13), the *temple in the Celle area* was sacred to Juno Curitis. The fine fronton statue of a draped female figure displayed here, possibly a goddess, dates to the mid-4th century restructure when the first, Archaic period *sacellum* was incorporated into a larger structure.

/madlb/

## LATIUM VETUS SECTION

**Rooms 32-34**

*Alatri, Ardea, Tivoli, Lanuvio, Segni, Gabi*

### Room 32

Here we find material brought to light with the first systematic excavations carried out in *Latium* as from the closing decades of the 19th century, along with the most significant of the happy chance finds of that period. Background to almost all these items was that vast panorama of sacred buildings of monumental inspiration extending

Fig. 68. Lanuvio, Temple of *Juno Sospita*. Antefix in the form of a female head with openwork nimbus. Ca. 500 BC.

gifts offered up to the divinity by devotees, possibly containing thousands of objects, most of which attested as being in wide circulation. Good examples are provided by the offerings found in the *temple* that rose outside *Alatri* (Lat. *Aletrium*) and in the *Pescarella district votive deposit* on the limits of the *Ardea* (Lat. *Ardea*) area and datable between the 4th and 2nd centuries BC. Peculiar to the *Latium* deposits, on the other hand, are the miniaturised, somewhat roughly hand-crafted objects of common use, deposited in the sanctuaries in great quantities as from the Orientalizing period. This particular category of votive offerings is exemplified by the *Tivoli* (Lat. *Tibur*) *votive deposit*

Fig. 69. Velletri, Colle Ottone district. Small clay model of a building. Archaic Age.

over the entire central Tyrrhenian area as from the 6th century BC, whose various features they reveal. Reflecting cult practices are the votive deposits – accumulations of

Fig. 70. Segni, acropolis temple. Fragment of a fronton high-relief depicting a warrior. Early decades of 5th century BC.

78

of *Acquoria*, which also included figurines cut out from bronze laminae – another type of gift characterising votive offerings in Archaic *Latium*. By way of contrast, the building industry is represented by a number of antefixes in the form of female heads, documenting the exceptional quality attained by Etruscan-Italic terracotta work in the Late Archaic Age. Outstanding is the splendid example with openwork nimbus that decorated the *temple* (*fig. 68*) of *Juno Sospita* at *Lanuvio* (Lat. *Lanuvium*). An exceptional gift was the small clay model of a building with double weathering, probably a temple structure, found at *Velletri* (Lat. *Velitrae*) (*fig. 69*). Representing the same cultural *koine* characterising the gifts to divinities in the Etruscan-Italic sanctuaries of the Archaic and Hellenistic Age is the material from the temple of *Juno Moneta* rising on the acropolis of *Segni* (Lat. *Signia*). Of the architectural elements decorating the building in its various constructional phases particular interest attaches to the remains of the *fronton high relief* (*fig. 70*) from the Late Archaic temple (500/480 BC) presenting a truly complex scene including at least three pairs of duelling warriors. Only one *funerary context* is displayed in this room, found in 1899 in the necropolis of the *Osteria dell'Ossa* district, in one of the burial grounds of the Latin city of *Gabii*. On the evidence of the quality vessels included in the grave goods and the use of a sarcophagus fashioned from an oak trunk the deceased must have belonged to the aristocratic class of *Gabii* in the 7th century BC.

/mgb/

THE TEMPLE OF ALATRI

Between the nymphaeum and the right wing of the Museum the *Etruscan-Italic temple of Alatri* rises in life-size reconstruction in the garden of the villa. Closely bound up with the events leading to the birth of the Museum itself, the work was completed between 1889 and 1890 on the basis of the remains of a sacred building datable between the 3rd and 2nd century BC, brought to light in Alatri – a town in *Latium* – between 1882 and 1885. The temple shows the characteristics of Vitruvius' Tuscan type and construction was evidently in two successive phases: an original nucleus consisting of the *cella* with a *pronaos* before it and, subsequently, a portico like that on the facade added to the rear of the building. The rich decoration of the temple is evidenced by the polychrome architectural terracotta fragments and antefixes (room 32) that once adorned the entablature and fronton weathering. Over and above philological considerations, this reconstruction stands as one of the earliest experiments in outdoor museum display of an archaeological complex, while also lending itself to didactic purposes.

/amms/

## Satrico

### Room 33

The ancient site of Satrico (Gr. *Satrikon*, Lat. *Satricum*) is of exceptional importance from the archaeological and historical viewpoint. Situated near the modern town of Borgo Le Ferriere, Latina province, the acropolis was frequented as early as the Bronze Age, while the period from the 9th to early 7th century saw a village of about thirty huts developing there. The *fine ceramics* and *luxury furnishings* (in ivory) contained in the dwellings offer confirmation at the everyday level of an aristocratic lifestyle becoming the pattern here, as amply attested by the *grave goods* found in the necropolis. The social status of the dead, including personages of princely rank (*tomb II* in the north-west necropolis), was also asserted with bronze furnishings (*fig. 71*) – some of which imported – in the funerary contexts, as well as an exceptional quantity of amber pieces and some fine tableware. The nerve centre of the site was the sanctuary dedicated to *Mater Matuta*, raised in the southern part of the acropolis and characterised by complex stratigraphy. The initial phase of the complex (last quarter of the 8th century – third quarter of the 6th century BC) is represented by an oval hut identified as the divinity's first dwelling place, associated with which was an open-air ditch to contain the votive offerings (*Archaic votive deposit*) filled with a great quantity of ceramics (of Greek and Etruscan importation as well as local production) and a great many objects in bronze, confirming the female nature of the divinity worshiped. On the hut site a sacellum with stone foundations was first constructed, and subsequently on the remains of this core the great Late Archaic temple was erected, building work going through numerous phases the precise chronology of which is still much debated among scholars.

Fig. 72. Satrico,
*Mater Matuta*
sanctuary, temple
II. Fronton high-
relief with the
head of a dying
warrior. Early
decades of 5th
century BC.

The notable *polychrome high relief from the fronton* (*fig. 72*)(490/480 BC) with the Greek myth of the Amazonomachy were installed with the renewed monumental organisation of the temple (so-called Temple II). The final phases in the life of the sanctuary (4th-2nd century BC) are documented, among other things, by the thousands of votive offerings filling the large ditch constituting the so-called *recent votive deposit*.

*Palestrina*

**Room 34**

The modern town of Palestrina occupies the site of the ancient Latin city of *Praeneste* (Gr. *Praineston*) to the south-east of Rome. Although the earliest archaeological evidence refers to phase II B in the protohistory of *Latium* (late 9th century BC), it was only between the late 8th and mid-7th century BC (phase IV A) that the centre saw development worthy of note. Its prosperity

81                                    *[mgb]*

must surely have had to do with the particular position it occupied: dominating the Latin-Sabine route to central-northern Italy, Praeneste enjoyed special relations with both the Etruscan world and the Italic hinterland as far as the Adriatic sea. The city's golden period is attested by the "princely" Barberini, Bernardini, Castellani and Galeassi tombs offering exceptional evidence of Orientalizing culture consisting of eastern (through the intermediation of the Etruscan cities of Cerveteri and Vetulonia), Etruscan and local products. To illustrate the magnificence attained by the local elites this room houses the grave goods from the Barberini and Bernardini tombs, found in the latter half of the 19th century. In the case of the *Barberini tomb*, we have no knowledge of the type or number of occupants, nor of the way the grave goods were arranged. Evidently it was the burial place of a warrior chief, datable between 670 and 650 BC, notable among the grave goods being the *throne* (*fig. 73*), *shield* and the *urn on a stand* (*fig. 74*), entirely fashioned in bronze lamina. Exceptional, too, are the ivories and jewellery, with such interesting items as the three-barred and comb-style fibulae and the singular plaque with sculptural decoration matched by a similar example from the *Bernardini tomb* (*fig. 75*). This latter tomb of a high-ranking warrior was of the ditch type

Fig. 73. Palestrina, Barberini tomb. Throne in bronze lamina. 670/650 BC.

Fig. 74. Palestrina, Barberini tomb. Bronze lamina urn on a stand. 670/650 BC.

82

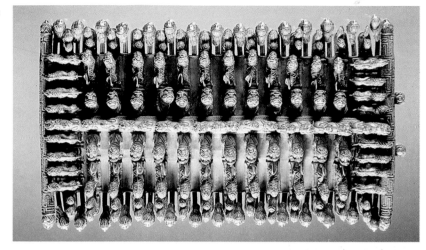

and yielded particularly rich grave goods consisting of *precious vessels* and *jewellery* datable between 680 and 650 BC. The grave goods were deposited in a ditch adjacent to the ditch in which the dead warrior's body was laid with his personal adornments. Apart from the great bronze urn on a stand it is also worth noting the gold *kotyle*, a small cauldron with serpent protomes (*fig. 76*), the *phialai* (*fig. 77*) and the goblet bearing the inscription *vetusia* (probably Latin, but with an Etruscan turn), all in silver, and a rare bowl in blue glass.

Between the late 6th and mid-5th century BC imports from Etruria reached a new high (jewellery, mirrors and various other furnishings in bronze). Thanks to contacts with the Etruscan master craftsmen, some certainly working in *Preaneste* itself by now, a flourishing local production developed in *cistae*, mirrors and bronze strigils, reaching a peak between the 4th and 3rd century BC. A good many of the items were found in the Colombella necropolis – in use between the 4th and early 1st century BC – subsequently entering the *Barberini Collection* and, with a few rare exceptions, we have no context for them.

As we know from other finds, the mortal remains were laid in sarcophagi (inhumation) and smaller caskets (cremation). In terms of ritual and culture the grave goods show a striking uniformity. The female burials are characterised by a mirror, the male burials by various, often related elements (spearheads, strigils, etc.). Typical of the grave goods are the *cistae* (containers for personal toiletry items such as combs, mirrors, cosmetics and perfumes), *mirrors, openwork vases* (containing a small leather pouch of oil mixed with

Fig. 76. Palestrina, Bernardini tomb. Small silver urn with serpent protomes. Second quarter of $7^{th}$ century BC.

Fig. 77. Palestrina, Bernardini tomb. Silver phiale. Second quarter of $7^{th}$ century BC.

84

pumice to wipe onto the body for cleansing purposes) (*fig. 78*), *strigils* (spoons used to scrape off the oil applied to the skin) and small animal-shaped wooden boxes containing rouge (crumbled cinnabar) and small pieces of sponge.

As from the late 3rd-early 2nd century the landscape of Palestrina was to be characterised by the grandiose proportions of the sanctuary of Fortuna Primigenia.

*/la/*

## UMBRIA SECTION                                    Room 35

*Terni, Nocera Umbra, Gualdo Tadino, Todi*

The important Umbrian collections were assembled between the late 19th and early 20th centuries, when the Museum collections covered a far wider area.

A good example of the pains taken by the Museum staff to safeguard scientific standards is the excavation of an extensive *necropolis* (10th-4th century BC) found in the course of works for the *Terni steelworks*. The grave goods displayed are from the most interesting phase in the life of the burial ground (10th/8th century BC). Among the richer, ditch burials with stone circles, the presence of weapons in some of the men's tombs and the display of ornaments in the women's reveal the beginnings of class differentiation, with the warrior chiefs occupying the highest social levels.

The Boschetto-Ginepraia necropolis (7th-6th century BC) lies in the heart of the Apennines, excavation being carried out in this virtually inaccessible area to the north of *Nocera Umbra* (Lat. *Nuceria*) in the early years of the 20th century. Among the grave goods displayed note in particular the two richest tombs of this small community, the so-called *tomb "of the little girl"* and *tomb 9*, also for a female, and possibly related, occupant.

Bordering with the territory of Nuceria was that of the Tadinati, mentioned in the Igvium (Gubbio) Tables, occupying the *Gualdo Tadino* area. The grave goods displayed here are from

the necropoleis of Malpasso and delle Cartiere, which served a community flourishing as from the 5th century BC, dominated by a warrior aristocracy (calotte-type helmets, curved broadswords). A peculiarity here is the presence of bronze-banded wooden kegs used to transport liquids (water, wine).

The discoveries made at *Todi* (Umbrian *Tutere, Tuter, Tute*, Lat. *Tuder*) are documented by various contexts including, notably, the two most important sets of grave goods from the Todi necropolis. The *warrior's tomb* in the S. Raffaele area (late 5th century BC) yielded not only a wealth of bronze banqueting ware and an extraordinary set of Attic ceramics, but also the impressive Attic-style ceremonial helmet in bronze damascened in silver and

86

Fig. 80. Todi, Pechiera necropolis, "tomb of the golden jewels". Pair of gold earrings with pendants in the form of female heads. First half of 3rd century BC.

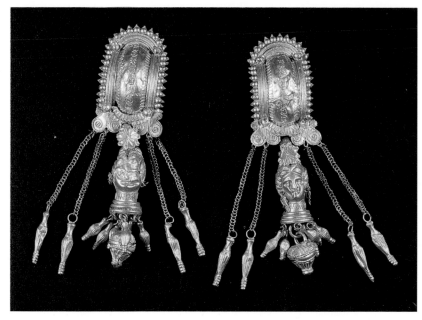

decorated with embossed battle scenes (*fig. 79*), of Vulci production. The *tomb of the "gold ornaments"* in the Peschiera necropolis, dating to the 3rd century BC, was the last resting place of a richly-clothed woman with a parure of gold ornaments of Etruscan production, notable among which are the necklace with *bulla* pendants and a pair of large earrings with pendants in the form of a woman's head (*fig. 80*). A particularly fine piece is the mirror incised with the scene of the judgement of Paris, and quite exceptional the set of figured bronzes (ansate patera, spouted oinochai, caryatid thymiaterion).

*/madbl/*

87

# BIBLIOGRAPHY

The relevant bibliography is indeed vast, and the following notes are intended to provide readers with reference above all to monographs addressing particular aspects of Etruscan civilisation in their entirety. Developments in study and research can be followed through specific articles contained in *Studi Etruschi*, a publication of the *Istituto Nazionale di Studi Etruschi ed Italici* that has been coming out annually since 1927, and in the proceedings of the meetings organised by the same Institute. Indispensable sources are to be found in the entries of the *Enciclopedia dell'Arte Antica, Classica e Orientale*, Rome 1958 ff., and in specialised publications such as *Bibliografia topografica della colonizzazione greca in Italia e nelle Isole tirreniche*, Rome-Pisa, and the *Lexikon Iconographicum Mythologiae Classicae*, Z_rich-M_nchen 1983 ff, abbreviated below as *EAA*, *BTGCI* and *LIMC*, which also have updated exhaustive bibliographies.

## GENERAL STUDIES

M. PALLOTTINO, *Etruscologia*, 7th ed, Milan 1984; M. CRISTOFANI, *Gli Etruschi Cultura e Società*, Novara 1978; M. Cristofani (ed.), Gli Etruschi. *Una nuova immagine*, Florence 1984; M. CRISTOFANI (ed.), *Civiltà degli Etruschi* (exhibition catalogue, Florence 1985), Milan 1985; J. BONFANTE (ed.), *Etruscan Life and Afterlife*, Detroit 1986; G. PUGLIESE CARRATELLI (ed.), *Rasenna. Storia e civiltà degli Etruschi*, Milan 1986; H.

Heres (ed.), *Die Welt der Etrusker, Internationales Kolloquium, Berlin 1988*, Berlin 1990. For rapid consultation, M. CRISTOFANI (ed.), *Dizionario Illustrato della civiltà etrusca*, Florence 1999.

## PROTOHISTORY AND THE PROTOURBAN FORMATIONS

F. DI GENNARO, *Forme di insediamenti tra Tevere e Fiora dal Bronze finale alla prima età del ferro* (Biblioteca di Studi Etruschi, 14), Florence 1986; G. BARTOLONI, *La cultura villanoviana. All'inizio della storia etrusca*, Rome 1989, and, in general, with reference to the first archaeological facies of the Early Iron Age: R. PERONI, *Preistoria e protostoria dell'Italia continentale. La penisola italiana nell'Età del bronzo e del ferro*, in Popoli e Civiltà dell'Italia Antica, IX, Rome 1989, p. 393 ff; R. PERONI, *Introduzione alla Protostoria italiana*, Bari-Rome 1994, *passim*; R. PERONI, *L'Italia alle soglie della storia*, Rome-Bari 1996 *passim*.

## HISTORICAL ASPECTS

In general:
M. TORELLI, *Storia degli Etruschi*, 2nd ed., Bari 1985, and for a picture of Etruscan history within the broader Italic context, M. PALLOTTINO, *Storia della prima Italia*, 3rd ed., Milan 1985.
Legends of the origins:
D. BRIQUEL, *L'origine lydienne en Italie*, Rome 1981.
The Archaic Age and relations with Rome:

J. HEURGON, *Il Mediterraneo occidentale della preistoria a Roma arcaica* (It. trans.), Rome-Bari 1986; M. CRISTOFANI (ed.), *Etruria e Lazio arcaico*, Atti dell'Incontro di studio (QuadAEI, 15), Rome 1987, M. CRISTOFANI, *La grande Roma dei Tarquini* (Exhibition catalogue , Rome 1990), Rome 1990.
The Roman conquest:
W.V. HARRIS, *Rome in Etruria and Umbria*, Oxford 1971; M. TORELLI, *Elogia tariquiniensai*, Florence 1975; A. CARANDINI, (ed.), *La romanizzazione dell'Etruria: il territorio di Vulci* (Exhibition catalogue, Orbetello 1985), Milan 1985.
The Etruscans in Campania:
M. FREDERIKSEN, *Campania*, Oxford 1984; *La Campania fra il VI e il III sec. a. C.*, Atti del XIV Convegno di Studi etruschi ed italici, Benevento 1981; Galatina 1992; *La presenza etrusca nella Campania meridionale*, Atti delle Giornate di Studio, Salerno-Pontecagnano 1990 (Biblioteca di Studi Etruschi 28), Florence 1994.
The Etruscans north of the Apennines:
G. BERMOND MONTANARI (ed.), *La Romagna tra VI e IV sec. a.C. nel quadro della protostoria dell'Italia centrale*, Atti del Convegno, Bologna 1982, Imola 1985; G. BERMOND MONTANARI (ed.), *La formazione della città in Emilia Romagna* I-III, Bologna 1987-88; L. MALNATI, V. MANFREDI, *Gli etruschi in Val Padana*, Milan 1991.

## ECONOMY AND SOCIETY

Settlement and exploitation of resources:

G. Schmiedt, *Atlante aerofotografico delle sedi umane in Italia. II. Le sedi scomparse*, Florence 1970; M. Cristofani, *Città e campagna nell'Etruria settentrionale*, Novara 1976. T. W. Potter, *The Changing Landcsape of South Etruria*, London 1979; *L'Etruria mineraria*, Atti del XII Convegno di Studi etruschi ed italici, Florence-Populonia-Piombino 1979, Florence 1981; M. Cristofani (ed.), *Gli etruschi in Maremma. Popolamento e attività produttive*, Milan 1981; G. Camporeale, L'Etruria mineraria (Exhibition catalogue, Portoferraio, Populonia, Massa Marittima 1985), Milan 1985; G. Barbieri (ed.), *L'Alimentazione nel mondo antico. Gli Etruschi* (exhibition catalogue, Viterbo 1987), Rome 1987.
Thalassocracy and commerce:
M. Cristofani, *Gli Etruschi del mare*, Milan 1983; M. Giuffrida Ientile, *La pirateria tirrenica. Momenti e fortuna* (*Kokalos*, suppl. 6), Rome 1983; Il commercio etrusco arcaico, Atti dell'Incontro di studio, Roma 1983; Roma 1985; M. Gras, *Trafics tyrrhéniens archaiques*, Rome 1985; M.A. Rizzo, *Le anfore da trasporto e il commercio etrusco arcaico. I. Complessi tombali dell'Etruria meridionale* (exhibition catalogue, Rome 1984), Rome 1990 (Studi di Archeologia published by the Soprintendenza Archeologica per l'Etruria meridionale, 3).
Coinage:
*Contributi introduttivi allo studio della monetizzazione etrusca*, Atti del V Convegno del Centro internazionale di studi numismatici, Naples 1975 (*Annali dell'istituto Italiano di Numismatica*, XXII, suppl.), Naples 1977; F. Catalli, *Monete etrusche*,

Rome 1990.
Institutions:
B. Liou, *Praetores Etruriae XV populorom*, Brussels 1969; M. Cristofani, *Società e istituzioni nell'Italia preromana, in Popoli e Civiltà dell'Italia antica*, 7, Rome 1978, pp. 53-112.
Religion:
R. Bloch, *Les prodiges dans l'antiquité*, Paris 1963 (It. trans. *Prodiigi e divinazione nel mondo antico*, Rome 1976); R. Herbig, E. Simon, *Götter und Dämonen der Etrusker*, Mainz 1965, 2nd ed.; G. Dumézil, *La religion romaine archaïque*, Paris 1966; A. Rallo, *Lasa Iconografia ed esegesi*, Florence 1974; A.J. Pfiffig, *Religio etrusca*, Graz 1975.
Everyday life:
J. Heurgon, *La vie quotidienne chez les Etrusques*, reprint, Paris 1979; L. Bonfante *Etruscan Dress*, Baltimore-London 1975; S. Steingräber, *Etruskische Möbel*, Rome 1979; E. Macnamara, *Vita quotidiana degli Etruschi*, Rome 1982; J.-P. Thuillier, *Les jeux athlétiques dans la civilisation étrusque*, Rome 1985; M.A. Rallo, *Le donne in Etruria*, Rome 1989; *Spectacles sportifs et scéniques dans le monde étrusco-italique*, Actes de la table ronde 1991, Rome 1993.

Architecture and artistic production:

In general:
M. Pallottino, *Civiltà artistica etrusco-italica*, Florence 1971 (reprint 1985); R. Bianchi Bandinelli, A. Giuliano, *Etruschi e Italici prima del dominio di Roma*, Milan 1973; R. Bianchi Bandinelli, M. Torelli, *L'arte dell'antichità classica. II. Etruria-Roma*, Turin 1976; M. Sprenger, G. Bartoloni, *Die Etrusker Kunst und*

*Geschichte*, Munich 1977; O. J. Brendel, *Etruscan Art*, Harmondsworth 1978; M. Cristofani, *L'arte degli Etruschi. Produzione e consumo*, Turin 1978; F.-H. Massa-Pairault, *Recherches sur l'art et l'artisanat étrusco-italique à l'époque hellénistique*, Rome 1985; M. Torelli, *L'arte degli Etruschi*, Bari 1985; G. Colonna, entry *Etrusca Arte, in Enciclopedia del'Arte Classica e Orientale*, Second Supplement 1971-1994, II, Rome 1994, pp. 554-605.

Towns and architecture:
G.A. Mansuelli, *La civiltà urbana degli Etruschi, in Popoli e civiltà dell'Italia antica*, III, Rome 1974, pp. 289-300; A. Boëthius, *Etruscan and Early Roman Architecture*, Harmondsworth 1978; F. Prayon, *Frühetruskische Grab- und Hausarchitektur*, Heidelberg 1975; Various Authors, *Strade degli Etruschi. Vie e mezzi di comunicazioni nell'antica Etruria*, Milan 1985; S. Stopponi (ed.), *Case e palazzi d'Etruria* (exhibition catalogue, Siena 1985), Milan 1985; G. Colonna (ed.), *Santuari d'Etruria*, (exhibition catalogue, Arezzo 1985), Milan 1985; *Architettura etrusca nel Viterbese. Ricerche svedesi a S. Giovenale e Acquarossa, 1956-1986* (exhibition catalogue, Viterbo 1986), Rome 1986; M. Bergamini (ed.), *Gli Etruschi maestri di idraulica*, Perugia 1991; M. Rendeli, *Città aperte*, Rome 1993.
Painting:
G. Colonna, entry *Tarquinia* in EEA, Supplement 1970, Rome 1973, p. 619 (with prec. bibl.); S. Steingräber (ed.), *Catalogo ragionato della pittura etrusca*, Milan 1985; *Pittura etrusca. Disegni e documenti del XIX secolo dall'archivio dell'Istituto*

*Archeologico Germanico* (exhibition guide, Tarquinia 1986), Rome 1989 (Studi di Archeologia published by the Soprintendenza Archeologica per l'Etruria meridionale, 2); M. A. Rizzo (ed.), *Pittura etrusca al Museo di Villa Giulia nelle foto di Takashi Okamuna* (exhibition catalogue, Rome 1989), Rome 1989 (Studi di Archeologia published by the Soprintendenza Archeologica per l'Etruria meridionale, 6); A. Naso, *Architetture dipinte. Decorazioni parietali non figurate nelle tombe a camera dell'Etruria meridionale (VII-V se. a.C.)*, Rome 1996.
Sculpture:
R. Herbig, *Die jüngeretruskischen Steinsarkophage*, Berlin 1952; A. Hus, *Recherches sur la statuaire en pierre étrusque archaïque*, Paris 1961; M. Cristofani, *Statue-cinerario chiusine di età classica*, Rome 1975; *Corpus delle urne ertrusche di età ellenistica. Urne volterrane*, I (M. Cristofani, ed.), Florence 1975; *Urne volterrane*, 2.1 (M. Cristofani, ed.), Florence 1977; *Urne volterrane*, 2.2 (G.Cateni, ed.), Pisa 1985; A. Maggiani, *L'Etruria settentrionale interna in età ellenistica* (exhibition catalogue, Volterra/Chiusi 1985), Milan 1985.
Terracotta sculpture:
A. Andrén , *Architectural terracottas from Etrusco-Italiac Temples*, Lund-Leipzig 1939-40; R. D. Gempeler, Die etruskische Kanopen Herstellung, Typologie, Entwicklungsgeschichte, Küssnacht 1974; P.J. Riis, *Etruscan Types of Heads. A revised Chronology of the archaic and classical Terracottas of Etruscan Campania and central Italy*, Copenhagen 1981; M.

Bonghi Jovino, *Artigiani e botteghe nell'Italia preromana. Studi sulla coroplastica di area etrusco-laziale-campana*, Rome 1990; *La coroplastica templare estrusca tra il IV e il II a.C.*, Atti del XVI Convegno di Studi etruschi e italici, Orbetello 1988, Florence 1992: E. Rystedt, Ch. and Ö. Wikander (eds.), *Deliciae Fictiles. Proceedings of The First International Conference on Central Italic Architectural Terracottas*, Rome 1990, Stockholm 1993; M.D. Gentili, *I sarcofagi etruschi in terracotta di età recente*, Rome 1994; P. Lulof, E. M. Moormann (eds.), *Deliciae Fictiles. Proceedings of The Second International Conference on Archaic Architectural Terracottas from Italy held at the Netherlands Institute in Rome, 12-13 June 1993*. Amsterdam 1997.
Ceramics:
J. D. Beazley, *Etruscan Vase-Painting*, Oxford 1947; G. Camporeale, *Buccheri a cilindretto di fabbricazione orvietana*, Florence 1972; M. Bonamici, *I buccheri con figurazioni graffite*, Florence 1974; T.B. Rasmussen, *Bucchero Pottery from Southern Etruria*, Cambridge 1979; *Contributi alla ceramica etrusca tardo-classica*, Atti del Seminario, Rome 1984, Rome 1985; M. Martelli (ed.), *La ceramica degli Etruschi. La pittura vascolare*, Novara 1987; M.A. Rizzo (ed.), *Un artista etrusco e il suo mondo. Il Pittore di Micale* (exhibition catalogue, Rome 1988), Rome 1988 (Studi di Archeologia published by the Soprintendenza Archeologica per l'Etruria meridionale, 5); M. Bonghi Jovino (ed.), *Produzione artigianale ed esportazione nel mondo antico. Il bucchero etrusco*. Atti del

colloquio internazionale, Milan 1990, Milan 1993; J. Szilágyi, *Ceramica etrusco-corinzia figurata*, Florence 1992; M. Micozzi, *"White-on-Red". Una produzione vascolare dell'Orientalizzante etrusco*, Rome 1994; J. Szilágyi, *Ceramica etrusco-corinzia figurata*, part II, Florence 1998.
Bronze production:
J. Mayer-Prokop, *Die gravierten etruskischen Griffspiegel archaischen Stils*, Heidelberg 1967; A. Hus, *Les bronzes étrusques*, Brussels 1975; S. Haynes, *Etruscan Bronze Utensils*, London 1974, 2ⁿᵈ ed.; G. Pfister-Roesgen, *Die Etruskische Spiegel des 5. Jahr. V. Chr.*, Bern-Frankfurt 1975; G. Bordenache Battaglia, *Le ciste prenestine. I. Corpus*, 1-2, Rome 1979; E. Richardson, *Etruscan Votive Bronzes. Geometric, Orientalizing, Archaic*, Mainz 1983; S. Haynes, *Etruscan Bronzes*, London-New York 1985: M. Cristofani, *I bronzi degli Etruschi*, Novara 1985; F. Jurgeit, *Le ciste prenestine. II. Studi e contributi*, Rome 1986; M. Bentz, *Etruskische votivbronzen del Hellenismus* (Biblioteca di Studi Etruschi, 25), Florence 1992. See also the *Corpus Speculorum* (CSE), in publication as from 1981.
Jewellery and glyptics:
P. Zazoff. *Etruskische Skarabäen*, Mainz 1968; W. Martini, *Die etruskische Ringsteinglyptik*, Heidelberg 1971; M. Cristofani, M. Martelli, (eds.), *L'oro degli Etruschi*, Novara 1983; M. Scarpignato, *Museo Gregoriano Etrusco. Oreficerie etrusche arcaiche*, Rome 1985.

The language:

M. Cristofani, *Introduzione allo studio dell'etrusco*,

Florence 1977; R.A. STACCIOLI, *La lingua degli Etruschi*, Rome 1968.

THE VILLA GIULIA MUSEUM:

DELLA SETA, *Museo di Villa Giulia*, Rome 1918; E. STEFANI, *Il Museo Nazionale di Villa Giulia*, Rome 1934; R.. VIGHI, F. MINISSI, *Il nuovo Museo di Villa Giulia*, Rome 1955; R. BARTOCCINI, A. DE AGOSTINO, *Museo di Villa Giulia. Antiquarium e collezione dei vasi Castellani*, Milan 1961; W. HELBIG, *Führer durch die öffentlichen Altertümer in Rom*, III, Tübingen 1969⁴, 467-862; W. HELBIG, *Führer durch die öffentlichen Altertümer in Rom*, IV, Tübingen 1972⁴; M. MORETTI, *Il Museo di Villa Giulia*, Rome 1973: VARIOUS AUTHORS, *Nuove scoperte e acquisizioni in Etruria Meridionale*, Rome 1975; G. PROIETTI,(ed.), *Il Museo Nazionale Etrusco di Villa Giulia*, Rome 1980; F. BOITANI (ed.), *Museo di Villa Giulia*, Rome 1983.

On the Museum collections and individual display sections, see also:

G.Q. GIGLIOLI, *Corpus Vasorum Antiquorum, Italia. Museo Nazionale di Villa Giulia in Rome, I*, Milan-Rome 1925; G.Q. GIGLIOLI, *Corpus Vasorum Antiquorum, Italia. Museo Nazionale di Villa Giulia in Rome, II*, Milan-Rome 1926;

G.Q. GIGLIOLI, *Corpus Vasorum Antiquorum, Italia. Museo Nazionale di Villa Giulia in Rome, III*, Milan-Rome 1927; P. MINGAZZINI, *Vasi della Collezione Castellani*, Rome 1930; P. MINGAZZINI, *Catalogo dei vasi della Collezione Augusto Castellani* II, Rome 1971: M. MORETTI, *Tomba Martini Marescotti* (Quaderni di Villa Giulia, 1), Milan 1966; M.T. FALCONI AMORELLI, *La Collezione Massimo* (Quaderni di Villa Giulia, 2), Milan 1969; F. CANCIANI, F.W. VON HASE, *La tomba Bernardini di Palestrina*, Rome 1979; M.A. FUGAZZOLA DELPINO, *La civiltà villanoviana. Guida ai materiali della prima età del Ferro nel Museo di Villa Giulia*, Rome 1984; I. CARUSO, Collezione Castellani. Le ceramiche, Rome 1985; A.M. COMELLA, *I materiali votivi di Falerii*, Rome 1986; R.N. KNOOP, *Antefixa Satricana*, Assen 1987; I. CARUSO, *Collezione Castellani. Le oreficerie*, Rome 1988; VARIOUS AUTHORS, *The Southwest Necropolis of Satricum*, Amsterdam 1993; A.M. COMELLA, *Le terrecotte architettoniche del santuario dello Scasato a Falerii. Scavi 1886-1887*, Perugia 1993; D.J. WAARSENBURG, *The Northwest Necropolis of Satricum*, Amsterdam 1995; B. GINGE, *Excavations at Satricum*

*1907-1910*, Amsterdam 1996; P.S. LULOF, *The late archaic temple at Satricum*, Amsterdam 1996; G. COLONNA, (ed.), *L'altorilievo di Pyrgi. Dei ed eroi greci in Etruria*, Rome 1996; VARIOUS AUTHORS, *Le antichità dei Falisci al Museo di Villa Giulia*, Rome 1998; A.M. MORETTI SGUBINI (ed.), Euphronios epoiesen: *un dono d'eccezione ad Ercole Cerite* (exhibition catalogue, Rome 1999), Rome 1999. Finally, for practical guidance to the archaeological sites and museums of southern Etruria, see: M. TORELLI, *Etruria*, Rome Bari 1980; G. BARBIERI, *Viterbo e il suo territorio*, Rome 1991; I. CARUSO, *Civitavecchia e il suo territorio*, Rome 1991; M.A. DE LUCIA BROLLI *L'Agro falisco*, Rome 1991; M.A. DE LUCIA BROLLI, *Civita Castellana. Il Museo Archeologico dell'Agro falisco*, Rome 1991; A.M. SGUBINI MORETTI, *Tuscania. Il Museo Archeologico*, Rome 1991; G. GAZZETTI, *Il territorio capenate*, Rome 1992; A.M. SGUBINI MORETTI, *Vulci e il suo territorio*, Rome 1993; M. CATALDI, *Tarquinia*, Rome 1993; A. TIMPERI, I BERLINGÒ, *Bolsena e il suo lago*, Rome 1994; R. COSENTINO, *Cerveteri e il suo territorio*, Rome 1995; I BERLINGÒ, H. BROISE, V. JOLIVET, *Museo Archeologico Nazionale di Viterbo*, Milan 1997.

# CONTENTS